Two Worlds

A Family's Search for Its History, Identity, and Legacy of
Ancestors on Whose Shoulders They Stand

Parson's Porch Books

Two Worlds: The Captives and the Enslaved
ISBN: Softcover 978-1539694847
Copyright © 2016 by Rhoda C. Nixon

All rights reserved. No part of this book may be reproduced or transmitted in any form or by any means, electronic or mechanical, including photocopying, recording, or by any information storage and retrieval system, without permission in writing from the publisher.

Credits:

"Mr. Black", from A LIFE ON THE ROAD by Charles Kuralt, copyright 1990 by Charles Kuralt. Used by permission of G. P. Putnam's Sons, and imprint of Penguin Publishing, a division of Penguin Random House, LLC.

Letters used by permission by Quinerly Family Papers (#186), Special Collections Department, J.Y. Library, East Carolina University, Greenville, North Carolina, USA.

To order additional copies of this book, contact:

Parson's Porch Books
1-423-475-7308
www.parsonsporch.com

Parson's Porch Books is an imprint of Parson's Porch & Company (PP&C) in Cleveland, Tennessee. PP&C is an innovative company which raises money by publishing books of noted authors, representing all genres. All donations from contributors and profits from publishing are shared with the poor.

Why would anyone want to write a family history...our ancestors are all dead? Why should we care? That refrain is heard over and over again as people neglect and endeavor to get rid of their heritage, believing it to be "old stuff" that needs to be forgotten. But in this age of "knowing the price of everything and the value of nothing," there are those who innately know the value of family memory. In each family there seems to be someone called to find the ancestors, the "chosen one," who gathers the genealogy. And by the sheer act of finding the information, breathes life back into the lives of our loved ones who went before.

Family history is not something obscure or unimportant. Old letters, photographs, scrapbooks, the family bible, and many other things help us to recall our past and the history of our family and the communities they lived in. Family history comes alive when someone is able to not only read about the past, but is also able to visit the places, appreciate the images, touch the heirlooms, study the actual words and place your ancestors in given places, times and events.

Memories are an important part of all our lives. We learn from our past in order to achieve greater influence over our future. History serves as a model of not only who and what we are to be, but to learn what to embrace and what to avoid. Every day decision-making around the world is constantly based on what came before us.

No matter how long you research, family history is never finished. Black family history is especially hard to research because of the lack of records. But what we uncover shows the hardships and the joys in the lives of our ancestors. We get a sense of who they were and see traits passed down the years in our genes. By writing a family history you are leaving a written legacy, all of the things that quite literally make us who we are.

Bless you Rhoda...What a gift to give your children, born and unborn...roots and wings to fly.   Best Wishes, Roger Kammerer

To: Roger Kammerer, my treasured friend, my heartfelt thanks for a most reflective, beautiful, and inspiring opening for our book.

Wishing you God's Blessings, Rhoda.

Mr. Kammerer is a well-known genealogist, artist, and historian. He has authored or co-authored 21 books or booklets on genealogy records.

Albert Debnam
Book Cover Artist

Albert Debnam is a designer with his interests planted in both the illustration and architectural industries. With building projects in the areas of performance theater design and residential kitchen and bath renovation, Albert has enjoyed a diverse career in visual development, graphic design and marketing for architects, interior designers and real estate developers throughout the United States.

To: Al, my grandson,

I am so proud and appreciative of the artistic symbol you designed for the cover of this book. It portrays our ancestor's horrific past in a vivid and unique way.

Love, Grandma Rhoda

Dedications

It is with great honor and pride that I offer this book to our Bryant/George ancestors who suffered one of the most horrific enslavements known to humankind. Through perseverance and a faith in the God who freed the Israelites, they had the assurance that someday God would also free them. We are eternally blessed to have had ancestors who were outstanding models for us to follow. We fully recognize that it is upon their shoulders we now stand.

To: My parents, Susie and William Carrison (Willie), who taught me to love history and story-telling. I also offer you my thanks and appreciation for sharing with me the excitement of exploring the lives and generations of people who came before us and to use these mediums of history and narratives to share these events with others.

My father's (Willie) love of history as well as his desire for black men to have their rightful place in our society is evident in the following poem he composed.

Give the Black Boys a Chance

First we leave our civilian life then to camps we must go
Leaving Mother, Father, and Sweetheart behind
Then fight Kaiserism from our door, then drill continuously upon the fields
Tis pleasure to see the lads prance, "Oh Heaven! I pray to all the World
Just give the Black Boys a chance."

Next, trench warfare is taught each one, charging the enemy in every way.
With determination, they grasp every way to achieve victory without delay.
Throwing hand grenades is taught them too, and gas is used in advance.
"Oh Heaven! I pray to all the World,
Just give the Black Boys a chance."

Now the camp training is 'bout o'er. They are packing to go 'Over there.
As they draw near and near the shore, they sing, "What the devil do we care."
When landed, the boys are eager to see
The sights and sorrows round about France.
"Oh Heaven! I pray to all the World,
Just give the Black Boys a chance."

O'er the top, the Blacks will dash with ambition to catch the Hun;
Germany will never win 'against a bunch like this.
Why? For they ae fighters every one
Like monsters they'll cross the "No Man's Land."
Killing the enemies at every glance,
"Oh Heaven! I pray to all the World,
Just give the Black Boys a chance."

Thru Berlin, Blacks will stroll and yet "Down with the Kaiser Bill."
Someone will ask the question, "How?"
The answer will be "its God's will."
We want freedom and justice for all mankind
After victory is won with the lance.
"Oh Heaven! I pray to all the World,
Just give the Black Boys a chance."

Composed by Wm. H. Carrison
May 17, 1918

Dedicated to

My son, Gerald, my daughter, JoAnne,
Our Bryant/George Family and especially our Young People.

I leave you now with the last line of a poem, "On the Origins of Things" by Listervelt Middleton.

> "Minute by minute and hour by hour,
> as you lose your history you lose your power."

Table of Contents

Preface ... 11

Chapter One
Lighting the Flame ... 15

Chapter Two
An Open Door to Our History ... 19

Chapter Three
The Pursuit of Our African History ... 38

Chapter Four
Ghana, Ancestral Birth Place of Our George Family ... 49

Chapter Five
The Tie that Binds ... 59

Chapter Six
How It All Began: The Trans-Atlantic Slave Trade ... 80

Chapter Seven
Arrival in Hell ... 87

Chapter Eight
A Sankofa Moment in History ... 96

Chapter Nine
Two Worlds: The Captives and the Enslaved   105

Chapter Ten
The History and Legacy of Noah and his Family   125

Chapter Eleven
A New Era in History   140

Chapter Twelve
Edward and Rhoda George's Story, Inspired by Census Reports   151

Chapter Thirteen
The George Sisters Share Their History and Legacy   162

Chapter Fourteen
Our George Family's Legacy and New Bethel Baptist Church   174

Chapter Fifteen
The Bryant Family Pays Tribute to Our Achieving and Accomplished Adults   189

Chapter Sixteen
Our Ancestors' Legacy is in Good Hands   201
Our Young People Hold the Bryant/George Banner High

Preface

A Family Tells their Story of Challenge and Resilience from Slavery to the Present.

> *"...and your descendants shall be like the dust of the earth, and you shall spread abroad to the west and to the east and to the north and to the south; and by you and your descendants shall all the families of the earth bless themselves." (Genesis 28:14)*

My ancestors, born into slavery, suffered one of the most horrific cruelties against humanity ever recorded. Their determination to survive and to succeed, despite the atrocities inflicted against them, has deeply inspired my life's journey. To cope with their suffering, they sustained a deep and abiding faith in a God who could deliver them in this world and prepare them for the next. They endured their plight but never gave up the struggle or the hope for liberation and freedom.

Throughout my life, I have been deeply committed to the search for our family's history, identity, and legacy. This commitment has grown out of the tremendous respect and love for my ancestors who gave so much to the fabric of their New World. Once freed, they became outstanding citizens and gave extraordinary service in many areas of American life.

Today, their stories of enslavement are no longer untold struggles of a determined people. Their stories have evolved to include the successes and accomplishments of generations of outstanding descendants in a land that once enslaved them. It is with pride that I offer this book to tell their stories and to offer our gratitude because it is upon their shoulders that we now stand.

Our Ancestral History Comes Alive

So many of us still remember the book, *Roots*, by Alex Haley.[1] It presents us with a vivid and extraordinary search by Haley to find his African roots and to establish his ancestral identity. In June of 1976, the only fact my family knew about our history was that Rhoda Bryant married Edward George.

At that time, Lucinda Fox Ward (granddaughter of Rhoda Bryant and Edward George) gathered all the cousins she could find to the New York Sheraton Hotel. This is where the flame was lit and the mandate given to determine our history and our Bryant/George connections. (It would not be possible until much later to determine our African lineage.) What a venture and challenge this would prove to be.

Through the years, Lucinda traveled to North Carolina to visit the Bryant relatives in an effort to obtain their oral history, and I often accompanied her. At one point, under the sponsorship of our cousin, Rhoda Bryant Darden, a mini-family reunion was held in Ayden, North Carolina. I attended, along with Lucinda, cousins Alice and Betty George from New York, and all the local family members. We enjoyed a wonderful "fish fry."

Our Special Salute to Lucinda Fox Ward
Our Organizer and First Bryant/George Coordinator

---

[1] Haley, Alex, Roots: The Saga of an American Family, New York: Dell Publishing Company, 1974

Lucinda Fox Ward passed away on October 1, 1984 of cancer. However, before she died, she turned over all the family information in her possession to me. She asked that I accept her torch to lead the family in our quest to find out "who we are." I accepted Lucinda's mandate and became the next Family Coordinator of the Bryant/George Reunions. We established that our reunions would be held every other year.

Working on the family history was like looking for a needle in a haystack, or searching for pieces of a jigsaw puzzle. Family members screened notes found in family Bibles, writings on the backs of old pictures, and listened to family stories that were preserved from oral traditions. We searched archives, court records, and libraries in North Carolina. We screened census reports. It was a time for celebration whenever we found information that began to fill in the missing gaps in our family's history.

For over fourteen years we kept digging, and at the turn of the twenty-first century a Millennium Family Reunion was held in Greenville, North Carolina. Earl Fulcher, grandson of Edward George, was our Chairperson. This reunion helped our collective history to come alive. We now had a connection to the place where our American ancestors had been enslaved and lived long ago. Also, relatives of two of Edward's brothers who had gone to Liberia with the Marcus Garvey Movement were located and joined us for that memorable reunion.

In 2012, the Bryant/George Family Reunion, with eighty-one persons in attendance, marked a significant milestone in our history. This reunion was held at Ingleside at Rock Creek, a retirement community in Washington, D.C. The highlight of the Reunion was the completion of a two volume history of the Bryant/George Family, entitled *"Yesterday, Today, and Tomorrow."* This souvenir gift, which detailed the discovery of nine branches of our family, was given to each family member who attended. Our relatives were very pleased to learn about the evolution of our family from slavery to the present time. The completion of this historical research was a tremendous effort spearheaded by JoAnne Stanback, great granddaughter of Rhoda and Edward Dudley George and her committee.

The Steering Committee's Thank You to the membership said it best:

To Our Dear Family,

It has been our pleasure to serve as your 2012 Steering Committee for this Bryant/George Family Reunion. Over thirty-six years ago, Cousin Lucinda Fox Ward conceptualized this beautiful dream to gather together her grandparents' "Kin" and to unite them as one.

We believe each reunion has been a true blessing as we learned and celebrated "who we are" and how we have evolved. This year, we documented all nine branches of our rich and fascinating history. We are committed to strengthening these bonds and to filling in the gaps as we uncover each new leaf of our family tree.

We acknowledge with our deepest appreciation all who have traveled from far and near to share this weekend with us, and who have offered gifts, talents, and support. It is our prayer that the Lord will bless and preserve "Our Family." As we depart, we pray that we will continue to connect and unite with one another until our next reunion.

Thank you for coming and God be with you as you travel home.

Family Reunion Co-Chairs
Jason Smith - Great-Great Grandson of Rhoda Bryant
George and Edward Dudley George
Jestina Gray - Great-Great Granddaughter of Robert George

Steering Committee
Ronda Bryant
Albert Debnam
Rhoda Nixon: Family Coordinator
JoAnne Stanback
Videographer- Roland Bryant
Cover Artist – Kismet Sofia Debnam

Chapter One
Lighting the Flame

Africa, The birth place of Humanity and our Family's History

When I envision my ancestors, from my intensive research, I can see them living out their daily lives. I reimagine ancient drumbeats beckoning them to various community activities. Drumbeats signaling festive celebrations were the rhythmic percussion announcing special meetings or rituals. The echoes of more frenzied beats clearly vibrating were perhaps alerting the community to danger – informing them that an enemy was approaching. These drumbeats were a tool and communication medium, a telling component of the innovative and community-based functions of their time. 'Great Kingdoms such as Ethiopia, Meroe, Nubia, Kanen, Ghana, Mali, Songhai, and the Congo, with their great contributions, existed before and while Europe lay in its dark ages.'[1]

Black people have often been referred to as a "third world" people. However, our ancestors are of the first humans, and as confirmed in modernity, all subsequent human groups descend from us. It is an accepted scientific fact that civilization began on the continent of Africa.

Biblically and scientifically, Africa is the oldest of the continents, containing the earliest remains of man. In comparison, 'European civilization has been shown to postdate the temples of India, the building of the palaces of Nineveh, planting of the Hanging Gardens of Babylon, construction of the pyramids of Cheops and Cephren and the temples of Palmyra and Thebes.'[2]

In 1959, anthropologists Lois and Mary Leakey made a startling discovery in Olduvai Gorge, Tanzania in East Africa. The sisters, who dedicated their lives to the field of paleoanthropology and were part of a multi-generational family of fossil hunters, found the remains of a human skull and stone tools that were nearly two million years old. The Leakeys postulated that 'over a period of a million years, some early peoples left Africa and crossed into Asia, from there, their descendants or offspring fanned out to populate the [entire] world.'[3]

An article in *Our Africa*[4] confirms that the climate of Africa provided a positive environment conducive to the survival of its earliest inhabitants. Africa is extensive: the second largest continent (approximately three times the size of the United States), encompassing the world's largest desert (the Sahara) and the world's longest river (the Nile) is bordered by the Atlantic, Indian, and Mediterranean Oceans and benefiting from their resultant climate zones. An article, *How Man Began,*[5] concludes as follows:

> While many unanswered questions remain about when and where modern humans first appeared, human ancestors almost surely emerged from Africa's lush forest nearly 4 million years ago. The warm climate was right, animal life was abundant and that's where the oldest hominid fossils have been recovered

As Black people, we have witnessed deliberate misrepresentations and misconceptions of the truth, perpetuated and wholly exaggerated in society. Wild accusations have described us as inferior—lacking in intellect, passion, and creativity and have taught us to mistrust our own. These myths were created concurrent with our captives casting our people into slavery. This struggle against oppression continues today. Yet, our ancestors have blessed us with a great legacy. We stand on the shoulders of great civilizations that have been at the forefront of the achievements from which the world has benefited and to which we witness today. We must tell our young people to arm themselves with our history and take comfort and strength from the achievements of previous and current generations. We have much to be proud of, walking the path in the way that the ancestors' spirits have guided us.

Today, Our Ancient African History Comes Alive

In our time, as we explore the history, culture, and legacy of our ancient African civilizations, we find that their contributions not only attributed to the skill set of Africans shipped around the world as slaves but also contributed to the building of countries and economies in the new world. Their ability to adjust, contribute, and survive is the legacy of all subsequent generations of human beings. As such, Africa and Africans continue to impact our lives today.

The Kushite people are considered the first civilization. According to *The Black Past: Remembered and Reclaimed*[6,] Egypt, with its glorious history, is highly revered, but little is known about Kush. However, it is because of the close relationship that existed between the two Kingdoms—Egypt and the Kushite, that both flourished. Egypt became the conduit to bring to us the rich history of the Kushite people. The Kush kingdom was located along the Nile River. Kushites farmed the Nile River Valley, developed principles of engineering, employed irrigation systems, mined minerals and precious stones for trade, and developed and introduced iron metallurgy to the region, including gold processing. Kushites traded ivory, ebony, and incense with Egypt which in turn traded with other Mediterranean people. In addition to agriculture, mining, and trade, the Kushites valued art and were skilled in architecture and craftsmanship.

Three other great African kingdoms were Ghana, Mali, and Songhai. An article, *The Story of African/West African Kingdoms* [7] gives us pertinent information about these kingdoms: The kingdom of Ghana (physically situated near present-day Senegal and Mauritania) was founded at about 1000 AD. It was famous for gold and trans-Saharan trade. Mali was formed in about 1200 AD from part of the ancient Ghanaian kingdom and specialized in the gold and salt trades and farming. The kingdom of Songhai was the largest of these ancient African kingdoms and the last to exist. It was formed in the late 1400's AD as a result of military incursions and specialized in trade, farming, and animal husbandry.

How Will the Knowledge of Our Ancient History Challenge Us Today?

The ebb and flow of tides and time,
Brings the rise and fall of ancient civilizations.

And with each, there are stories of
Glory, failures, conflicts, and achievement.

Now we have the opportunity
To tell the stories of our time,
And the question is
How will the ebb and flow that defines us
Be viewed and judged by the generations
That will follow in our footsteps?

Endnotes

1. The Second Edition of National Geographic Magazine, Published 1889
2. Ibid.
3. The African American Experience- A History, Globe Book Company, p.4
4. Our Africa, (http://www.our-africa.org/climate)
5. How Man Began, Time: The Weekly Magazine, (March 14, 1994), p.83
6. Ancient Kush (2nd millennium B.C.-4th century A.D. / "The Black Past: Remembered and Reclaimed",
    http://www.blackpast.org/gah/ancient-kush-2nd-millennium-b-c-4th-century-d
7. The Story of African/West African Kingdoms, BBC World Service

Chapter Two
An Open Door to Our History

Throughout my life, I have been deeply committed to the search for our family's history, identity, and legacy. A commitment that has grown out of the tremendous respect and love for my ancestors who survived one of the most horrific enslavements in history, and yet gave so much to the fabric of their New World. After their emancipation, our ancestors became outstanding citizens and gave extraordinary service in many areas of American life. It is with pride that I offer this book to tell their stories and to offer our gratitude, because it is upon their shoulders that we now stand.

Memories and Oral Accounts that Shape Who We Are

As a little girl growing up, I was always excited when a trip was planned to visit my mother's relatives down south. I especially felt a connection to the farm where I was born. It was on the same land where our Bryant family had been enslaved. The farm was located in Henrahan, not far from the Townships of Ayden and Grifton in Pitt County, North Carolina.

I also had a special kinship and connection to my cousins who were about my age. We were brought into this world by a mid-wife who was carefully supervised by our Aunt Jane.

Aunt Jane's Test for New Babies

Through the years, one of Aunt Jane's traditional customs was to see if the new born baby could pass her test to become a family member and earn the title of "Tar Heel." R.B .Creecy tell us:

> ...that during the unhappy War Between the States, North Carolina was sometimes called the "Tar Heel State," because tar was made in the State, and in battle the soldiers of North Carolina stuck to their bloody work as if they had tar on their heels. When General Lee said, "God bless the Tar Heel Boys", (they and we assumed the name.)[1.]

End Note- 1. R.B. Creecy's Grandfather's *Tales of North Carolina History* (1901)

When I was born, it was my turn to have this ritual performed on me. Aunt Jane took a newly cooked sweet potato and mashed it until it was smooth and creamy. She then placed a little of the mixture on a spoon and placed it on my lips. I have been told, to the glee of everyone present, I smacked my lips after tasting the mixture. That's when Aunt Jane declared me an official family member and a real North Carolina tar heel.

Our Aunt Jane Bryant was called the family's matriarch. When I visited, as a child, she and other family members were sharecroppers and still worked for the Quinerly family, their former slave masters. The slave shacks had been taken away and new houses built with several rooms. Aunt Jane's "home place" as it was called became the central place for the family to drop by and to assemble.

Aunt Jane's Homeplace

Much of our oral history speaks about Aunt Jane who passed away about a year after I was born. Her granddaughter, Rhoda Jones Darden, accepted her mantle and became that nurturing spirit who offered us warmth, love, and wisdom. My earliest memories of my North Carolina family begin with her.

Our ancestral history begins with Noah, Jane, and Rhoda. These siblings were the only survivors to trace our Bryant's family tree. Rhoda Bryant George is my grandmother and many of the stories shared in this book will be about her. We will also have further stories about matriarch, Jane Bryant Jones. We will learn more about Noah, their older brother, who became a legend in Pitt County and throughout the area. People called him the "Teacher" because he risked his life to teach anyone, who desired to know, how to read and write.

Lucinda Fox Ward, as she started to explore our history, called us the Bryant/George Family. Oral memories indicated that her grandmother, Rhoda Bryant, was married to Edward Dudley George. In my attempt to confirm this, I searched marriage and cohabitation records in courts and local archives in North Carolina, but my efforts were not successful. Therefore, nothing else was known about our grandfather, other than that he was born in Jones County. This was confirmed by Lucinda's mother and my mother's birth certificates which indicated that their father Edward Dudley George's place of origin was Jones County.

I remember taking frequent trips to New York City to visit Lucinda and her mother, my Aunt Julia. It was there that I was introduced to many "Kin" folks. The word "Kin" indicated to us that we were relatives, but did not specify how or why. They had last names that I had not heard before. Their last names were Chadwick, Fulcher, Riddick, and Rhodes (spelled Rhoades by some family members). It remained a mystery to me for many years how those names and the people I met were connected.

A Picture is Worth a Thousand Words

In 2000, we began to consider the information that family members were bringing to our reunions. We enjoyed reviewing and trying to make sense of the bits and pieces. Yet, there was no concrete evidence to shed light on who we were and how we were connected. There was nothing to launch us on our way.

One of our relatives, Daniel Rhoades, joined us and was so excited to meet so many kin folks, and to be a part of our search to find our identity and history. His enthusiasm was contagious. Just being around Dan made you feel that we were on the road toward something big. He was encouraging and steadfast in feeling that we would be able to connect the bits and pieces together.

At a subsequent reunion, Dan brought a picture that his aunt, Addie Ferbuy, had given him. It was a picture of seven women. As we looked at the picture, excitement mounted in us. We each recognized someone in the picture that was connected to us. There was Fannie Fulcher, Sennie Riddick, Sallie Ann Rhoades, and Nettie Chadwick.

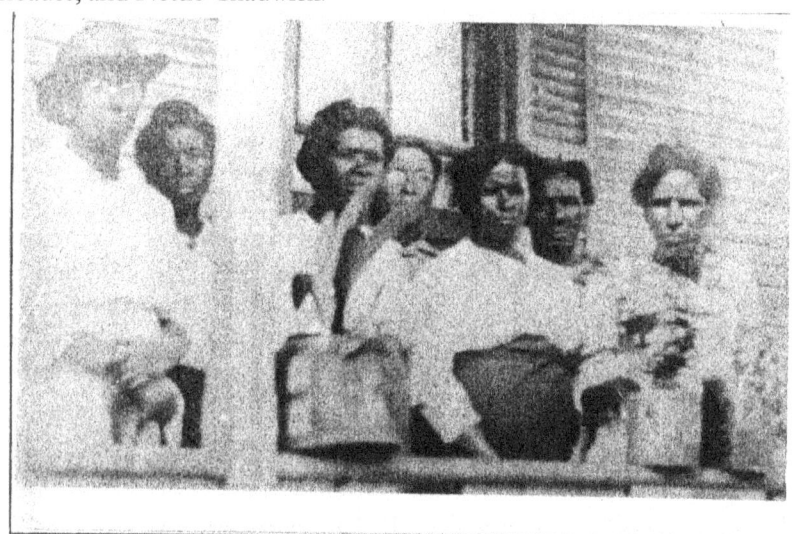

Fannie, Sennie, Sallie Ann, Friend, Nettie, Friend, Friend

We determined that these women were our grandmothers. We hugged one another and jumped with joy. The pieces of the puzzle were falling into place. We concluded that the women were the George sisters and realized that we really are cousins. The pictured showed that the woman on the extreme right was a friend of the sisters. We concluded that since there were only four George sisters, the other two persons on the back row were also friends.

Daniel Rhoades (Dan) and his sister, Mabel

Another Picture Sheds Light on Our Family History

Cousin Earl Fulcher has also been deeply involved in our research to determine the identity, history, and legacy of our ancestors. We shared his excitement when he found a picture that could also be a missing link to shed light on "who we are." His "find" would possibly usher in an earlier generation of our George family. Earl felt this picture of John George and Amy Kennedy George could be the parents of the five George brothers and the four George sisters.

Census reports now revealed that Johnnie was the oldest George brother. We learned from oral history that three of the George brothers: Samuel, Robert, and Nathaniel, had gone to Liberia in the early 1920's with the Marcus Garvey Movement. We were told that Nathaniel did not adjust to living in Africa and he returned home to North Carolina. The final and fifth male sibling, Edward Dudley, was Lucinda's and my grandfather.

As I prepared to share the picture of John, Amy George and a child, I realized that the picture probably is a drawing made from a photo. Note the fingers of Amy and the little girl in the picture as well as the narrow shoulders and exaggerated pants legs of John George. The person responsible for this drawing certainly demonstrates real artistic skill and ability, but also evidences difficulty in drawing fingers, proportion, and wrinkles in the man's pants.

The possibility that this picture is a drawing makes it a real miracle. It surely has stood the test of time. It also means that one of our kin folks, possibly enslaved, drew this picture. They have now given us a pictorial representation

JOHN GEORGE AND AMY KENNEDY GEORGE

for our family tree, a generation not previously known. We now accept this memorable gift with gratitude, love, and celebration.

Parents of

Edward Dudley George   Nettie George Chadwick
Johnnie George   Fannie George Fulcher
Robert George   Sallie Ann George Rhoades
Samuel George   Sennie George Riddick
Nathaniel George

My Aunt Millie, our Family Historian and Communicator

Aunt Millie George Carter, one of the oldest children of Rhoda and Edward Dudley George, was called our family historian. She was the glue that held us together. Aunt Millie and her husband, Edward [called Eddie,] always provided an open door for relatives and friends. People came for short visits or would drop by usually at meal time. Aunt Millie, who was a wonderful cook, provided delicious meals as if she always expected someone else to arrive. She said, "I have extra food in the pot, just in case."

When I was 12 years old, I lived for a year or more with my aunt and uncle. They assisted my father in taking care of me because my mother was ill. My mother, often called "little Susie," was the youngest of the sixteen children. It appeared to be Aunt Millie's role to step up when anyone had a problem. I returned home after my mother's recovery, but continued to be included in my aunt and uncle's activities. Aunt Millie usually told me when an important event was being planned, or when they were having special company. After getting permission from my parents, I packed my bag and moved in to be a part of the happenings.

I later studied Group Work (part of the Social Work program) in college, but I had the best Group Work teacher in my Aunt Millie. She was always creating and leading programs at our church, New Bethel Baptist. Other churches also asked for her help with their events, and Aunt Millie usually took me along. Sometimes, I had a role in the program; other times, she called me her assistant, which made me feel so important and proud.

Millie George Carter, her mother, Rhoda Bryant George, and her brother, Edward George, were Charter Members of New Bethel Baptist Church in Washington, D.C. Also pictured on the next page is Aunt Millie and Rev. C. David Foster, Church Pastor at that time.

Aunt Millie and C. David Foster, Pastor

A Link with Our Liberian Cousins Renewed

Although I was about sixteen years of age, I can still remember when I met one of our cousins from Liberia, Africa. I was attending a youth meeting at our church. Aunt Millie, who was also there, called me out of my meeting and introduced me to a tall, young man whose name was Sammy George. I had often heard the story of my Liberian cousins who had gone to Africa as a part of Marcus Garvey's "Back to Africa Movement." After emancipation, free and enslaved African-Americans faced continuous hardship and inequality. Marcus Garvey offered them an opportunity to seek a better life in Liberia. Aunt Millie kept in touch with our cousins in their new land and often told me about their life and progress in their new home.

I was so pleased to actually meet and see an African relative rather than to just hear about someone who lived in a far-away place. Aunt Millie shared that Sammy George had come to the United States to attend Law School. Then she proudly shared that Sammy, after receiving his law degree, planned to return to his country. He wanted to be an advocate for poor people and to give them appropriate legal representation in the courts. I was very impressed that Sammy would pursue such a noble cause.

Years later, I would find out from his grandniece, Jestina Gray, that the tall young man who I met at age sixteen did indeed achieve his noble cause. He became a renowned, respected, and brilliant lawyer. His desire to ensure that justice prevailed for all men, rich or poor, earned him the title: "Poor Man's Lawyer."

Samuel George truly did have compassion for the poor and underprivileged. He visited persons in the prison cells whom he felt were innocent and then represented them in the high courts. Otherwise, those inmates would have lingered in prison for years because they could not afford legal representation. His popularity as "the people's lawyer" earned him a seat in the House of Representatives for Montserrado County (Liberia), and later in life, the Honorable Samuel David George was a presidential candidate for the Republic of Liberia.

Alas, I Would Revisit My Relationship with Sammy George

It was the year 1965, and I was married to Joseph Todd who was from Liberia. His parents had also gone to Africa with the Marcus Garvey Movement. An aunt bought him to the United States when he was a teenager to attend high school, in preparation for college. Unfortunately, Joseph could not recall knowing my family, but indicated perhaps his brother, Alexander, who still lived in Monrovia might have known them. Alexander planned to visit us soon. I could barely wait for his brother's visit.

Time passed, and one day Joseph excitedly shared that his brother was on his way to visit us. I hoped and prayed that Alexander would be a connection to my family. I was not disappointed when his brother arrived. To my amazement, he did know my cousin Sammy George, by the populist term "Poor Man's Lawyer." He also knew that there were two George families in Monrovia, one from the United States and the other from the Caribbean. He thought I was most probably related to the George family from the United States. He was uncertain about the George family from the Caribbean.

My brother-in law indicated his plan to visit Sammy George, once he returned home and to have Sammy contact me. I was overjoyed by the possibility that I could be in touch with my Liberian cousins and also have contact with Sammy George again. I hugged Alexander over and over again for bringing me such good news.

I was ecstatic when my cousin Sammy George called me. He was in the United States attending a Lott Carey Baptist Convention. I remembered my mother talking about the Lott Carey Conventions of her time. Sammy also indicated his pleasure at being able to talk with me again. I was especially delighted that he remembered me. However, in future talks by phone, we had limited time to learn much about one another or my Liberian family. He usually called in between his meetings.

My last meeting with Samuel George, however, was a very meaningful one for me. He had heard from my former brother-in-law, Alexander, that my husband and I had divorced. Sammy was very protective and supportive. He encouraged me to go forward from that moment and make a fruitful life for myself and family.

The Honorable and Mrs. Samuel David George

After a period of time, I realized that I had not received any calls from my cousin Sammy. I would learn much later that the Hon. Samuel George had passed away from cancer. Aside from the pain of his death, I also had to face the crucial fact that I no longer had a connection to my African family. Although my contact and interactions with Sammy had been short-lived, the relationship was tremendously meaningful to me. It would now inspire me to a greater mission: to make every effort possible to find other members of my Liberian family.

That mission was accomplished when in 1996 cousins from two continents were gloriously reunited in a never-to-be-forgotten Bryant George Reunion in Norfolk, Virginia. The following news article chronicles this event.

Woman Revels in Finding Long-lost Family
Norfolk Metro News, July 20, 1996. Staff Writer, Wendy Grossman

Fannie Fulcher Jones is pictured with cousins Hashim Fulcher of Charlotte, NC (left) and Rick Fulcher of Atlanta, GA who were attending the third Bryant/George Reunion, which was held in Norfolk, Virginia. Cousin Fannie was Chairperson for the 1996 Family Reunion.

Cousin Fannie's picture and her remarks clearly showed her excitement about the family reunion being held that weekend. For the past month, she had been very busy, putting the finishing touches on her menu and table decorations, picking out her outfits, and polishing her welcome speech for her relatives.

She said, "There's a lot of catching up to do. Three cousins are from Monrovia, Liberia. Ten more African-born relatives have arrived from Maryland, New York, and Los Angeles. Most came to the United States in the early 1990's after the civil war in Liberia. At 62 years old, I'll be seeing relatives I've never seen in my life. Some I didn't know existed."

Fannie then shared how our family found their long lost relatives. She explained that a cousin, Rhoda Nixon, had been on a crusade to find her Liberian cousins. She asked every African person she met if they had knowledge of her cousins. Desperate to find them, Rhoda, who was a Presbyterian minister, considered contacting a Presbyterian church in Liberia. However, Liberia was once again plunged in a civil war and persons with close knowledge of the situation advised her against any contact with relatives there. The civil war had now spread from the countryside into Monrovia. Any inquiry about her relatives could endanger their lives. Saddened by this news, Cousin Rhoda focused on having our family in prayer for their safety.

Much later, Cousin Rhoda was pleasantly surprised when she met a former Ambassador to Liberia, Eugenia Stevenson, at a wedding. It was the wedding celebration of the daughter of Julia Cheeseman, one of Cousin Rhoda's church members. Rhoda and her former Liberian husband had been close friends of the Ambassador, who often visited their home and they also attended Embassy events. Cousin Rhoda was extremely delighted and excited when Ambassador Stevenson said that she not only knew her cousins but that they also live in Maryland. The Ambassador said she would contact them and arrange to have them call Cousin Rhoda.

The Honorable Ambassador Eugenia A. Stevenson

A few days later, Cousin Rhoda received a telephone call from a lady who said, "I am your Liberian cousin, Jestina Gibson." Cousin Rhoda could hardly restrain herself as she asked, "Where are you?" Jestina answered, "I live in Adelphi, Maryland". Cousin Rhoda immediately responded. "I live in Adelphi, Maryland, too." After Cousin Jestina said, "I live off of Riggs Road," Cousin Rhoda was barely able to catch her breath. "I live off Riggs Road, too." The two families lived less than 8 blocks away from one another!

Fannie also marveled at the thought that the Liberian cousins were now with us at this reunion and were feeling so welcomed by their Bryant/George family. She added that we have now united our two continents!

Fannie's Newspaper Story Launches Our Television Debut

Cousin Fannie's newspaper story prompted a call to me about a week after our reunion. The gentleman on the phone asked if I was the Rhoda Nixon in the newspaper article who found her long-lost relatives. After indicating that I was that person, he then shared that he was a producer who represented Channel 7, Lifetime Television. I couldn't believe it, a television producer, really? The gentleman continued to explain that Lifetime Entertainment

Services was presenting a program called Beyond Chance. I indicated that I was aware of the program and was a regular viewer.

He further explained that the producers were looking for additional persons with a story of a life-changing experience, a twist of fate that turned their lives in another direction. He felt my newspaper story showed that I had experienced a near-impossible event, one that was beyond chance; an event that brought my long-lost relatives into my life after years of searching for them.

The Producer shared that Grammy-winning musician, Melissa Etheridge, was hosting this hour of compelling true stories. She had sold more than 25 million records worldwide and had won numerous awards, including two Grammys. This gifted artist was also the recipient of the prestigious ASCAP Songwriter of the Year Award. Melissa had returned to the music scene with her album "Breakdown" after a three-year hiatus and also had taken on this exciting new opportunity as the story-telling host for *Beyond Chance*.

Beyond Chance had received Honorable Mention from the American Women in Radio and Television's Gracie Award in the Category of National/Syndication Reality Show and had been the recipient of congratulations and outstanding recognition.

The producer indicated that if I would agree to his organization's telling our story on television, his producer would contact me to make the necessary arrangements and tell me what was involved. Lifetime would contract a local television crew to help us re-enact our story. I contacted family members to obtain their input and to see how many people would be available to participate in our television debut. The rest is history.

For the next two years, our story was told and retold to Lifetime audiences. Often people would tell me, "I saw you on *Beyond Chance* last night. Other family members delighted in knowing that our story about finding our Liberian kinfolk was now available for others to see and to rejoice with us.

To give you a glimpse of our experience, the following pictures will show the television crew working with us.

From left to right: Leneh Ricks, family friend; Mama Jessie, our Liberian Family Matriarch; Mrs. Julia Cheeseman, the friend and church member mentioned earlier; Granddaughter Elizabeth Gray, her Mother, Jestina Gray, and Granddaughter Tysha Tolbert.

Mama Jessie greets Melvin, great grandson of Aunt Millie and Uncle Henry Williams, our youngest arrival in the family at that time, while others look on. Melvin's Mother-Tina (not shown) is also present at this event. Left to right: Elizabeth Gray, Michele Stanback, Baby Melvin, Jestina Gray and standing, Mama Jestina Gibson.

Seated is my son Gerald Smith, who is a Cultural Historian and Lecturer, and Matthew Stanback, my grandson.

This is a close-up of two camera crew members. Another male cameraman (not shown). Filming our "Beyond Chance" television Segment. Gerald is having a discussion with some of the young people, as Mama Jessie, Jestina, and I listen.

We had a wonderful celebration, and fellowship. Thanks to the *Beyond Chance* producers a delicious luncheon was enjoyed by all in attendance. This group picture was taken at the home of my daughter, JoAnne Stanback, in Mitchellville Maryland, who is on the extreme right.

Additional footage was taken in Adelphi, MD at my home as well as at the home of Cousin Clarise Tolbert (Daughter of Mama Jestina). Other family members not seen above were participants in the television segment.

At each family reunion we viewed and enjoyed the *Beyond Chance* CD, called "The Tie That Binds."

Memorial Tribute to an Extraordinary Cousin

Earl Fulcher and Wife, Sadie

Earl has been an ardent researcher, collaborating often with others to discover "who we are" as the Bryant/George family. His efforts helped identify Amy Kennedy and John George, who were born enslaved, as the beginning of the George family tree. During our 14-year research period, Earl was one of our most enthusiastic and vigilant leaders. His no-nonsense manner kept us on point and his love for us served as a unifying force.

At the turn of the century, we decided to return to the area where it all began. Therefore, we planned and held our 2000 Millennium Family Reunion in Greenville, NC. Earl was our Chairperson. It was a wonderful weekend filled with activities, a tour of the community, and worship at our family church. This reunion helped our collective history to come alive and to become more real for us. We now had a connection to our ancestors of long ago. This also was a great moment because our newly-found Liberian cousins were with us.

Our family held our July, 2008 Reunion in Laurel, MD. This special event honored our family patriarchs, one of whom was Earl. It was with great pride that we presented Earl with this special recognition. He was not only a pillar of strength for our family, but also in his many other endeavors.

Earl, son of Naomi Fulcher and Lucius Boney, was also the grandson of Fannie George Fulcher. He and his wife Sadie were married for 36 years and had two children, Jeffrey and Suzanne. Earl grew up and was educated in New York City. After high school, he served in the United States Air Force, and received an honorable discharge for his service. He then attended City College of New York where he majored in Science and Math and received a Bachelor of Science degree.

Earl subsequently received Masters' degrees in Guidance Counseling from Long Island University, and in Supervision and Administration from Baruch College, both in New York. Earl taught Math and other subjects for many years at Junior High School 58, in Brooklyn, and later was appointed the school's Assistant Principal. He also served a 10-year stint in Newark, New Jersey's Juvenile Parole System. In Earl's role as President of Freehold New Jersey's NAACP, he attempted to move the organization from one focused on reaction to situations to an organization that was proactive.

Earl saw his organizational life and our family as a "salad bowl" where each person could make his or her own distinct contribution, which contributed to the whole. Our prayers go out to his wife, Sadie, and children Suzanne and Jeffrey. We also pray that Earl's loving spirit will ever be near us, in the blessing of caring thoughts and in the comfort of cherished memories.

Love,

The Bryant/George Family

Earl B. Fulcher, January 16, 1932-May 15, 2013

Chapter Three
The Pursuit of Our African History

Our family has pursued a mandate for a number of years given to us by Lucinda Fox Ward who was the first family organizer. Her mandate has led us in various directions, and many family members have participated in this venture. We have searched family bibles and pictures and listened to stories from oral history. I have made countless trips to North Carolina, to East Carolina University, local courts and libraries, in Ayden and Durham North Carolina, in an effort to gain some understanding of "who we are" as a family. This has been an exhausting, lifelong, exciting study that has bonded us together in a common cause.

We have made great strides in this pursuit. However, there is one question that still eludes us: where is our birthplace in Africa?

Our slave holders were very successful in their use of extreme methods to destroy traces that would define us as a viable people with a significant and extraordinary history; a history that began with the earliest civilizations of human kind. The lives of our enslaved ancestors were so horrific that, once freed, they buried those experiences in their memory banks. They remained silent as they focused on day to day living and chose not to revisit or share those painful times.

Time always ushers in new information and new ideas which prompt the curious to examine conditions that have affected their lives. The discovery of DNA has proven to be an important contribution to the fields of biology and biomedical research. This discovery would also be an open door to our history in Africa.

Through DNA testing, I desired to discover the African origin of my Bryant/George ancestors. In 2013, a friend told me about African Ancestry, Inc. This is a program founded in 2003 by Dr. Rick Kittles and Gina Paige. I was informed about Dr. Kittles when he was a molecular biologist at Howard University, but was unable to contact him. At that time, his new ideas raised some doubts, but they were later found to be on the cutting edge of DNA technology.

African Ancestry Inc. is now considered a world leader in tracing maternal and paternal lineages of African descent. With the help of our cousin, Newton George, I was able to submit our DNA to see if there was a match from an ancient pool of DNA samples. We were extremely excited to have this opportunity and eagerly awaited the results.

The wait was rewarded with my receiving our Bryant ancestor's results (cited below). I called many of our family members to share the good news. We are now eagerly awaiting Newton's certificate to tell us about our George relatives' test results.

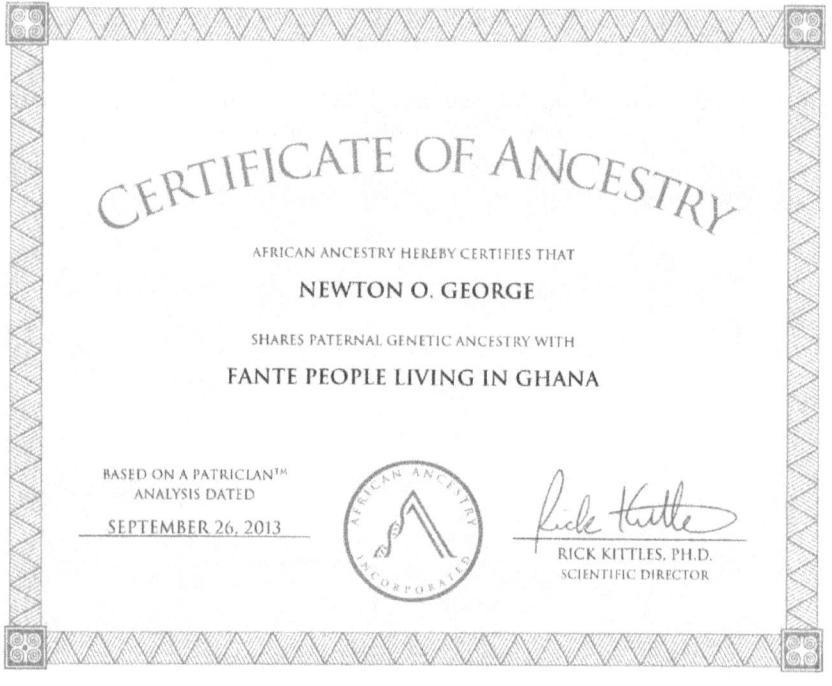

It was truly celebration time for our Bryant/George family. We experienced a feeling of immense joy to finally know where our roots lie in Africa. It was a real blessing to have an identity and a people that we could now call our own. To have maternal genetic ancestry with the Temne people of Sierra Leone and paternal genetic ancestry with the Fante (also spelled Fanti) people of Ghana links us with African ancestors whose histories we also share.

A flurry of activity ensued as our family members and I researched books, searched the internet, and compared notes with one another. We were jubilant!

Temne: The language of My People

I would like to share an interesting experience that has given me a glimpse into my Sierra Leonean ancestry. I have a goddaughter, Veda, who is from Ghana but has also lived in Liberia. Because Sierra Leone and Liberia share open borders with one another, their societies have adopted common customs and languages. Therefore, Veda and her family are fluent in our Temne language.

One day, Veda and one of her sisters, Abigail, and I were visiting together. They decided to let me hear them conversing in Temne, my ancestral language. The language was very pleasing to my ears, and I could fantasize myself centuries ago in an African village.

The two sisters then wanted me to join them in conversation and encouraged me to try out some simple greetings. I have never been able to quickly learn foreign languages and struggled in school with Latin and German. So I was hesitant to try, but they would not give up on me. To my surprise and to their glee, I was able to learn the greetings and remembered them. It was then that Veda and Abigail cheerfully concluded that I learned quickly because the Temne language is in my DNA.

After having this experience with my goddaughter and her sister, I desired to know more about my Temne relatives. My research described the Temne as a strong, aggressive warrior-like people who through the centuries migrated from ancient Israel to present day Sierra Leone. Because of their aggressiveness, trading, and business savvy the Temne have often, even today, been referred to as the "Black Jews." Guineelibe tells us that "according to some oral traditions, the history of the Temne migration toward present day Sierra Leone begins in ancient Israel. From Israel the Temne migrated to Ethiopia and from Ethiopia to the Mali Empire. After the Mali Empire, they migrated to Jalunkandu Empire in the 11th and 12th centuries, mainly due to the fall of the Jalunkandu Empire in what later became Fauta Jaillon, in the highlands of present-day Republic of Guinea."[1]. Historians also believed that the Temne were long distance kola nut traders when West Africa's trade was conducted across the Sahara Desert.

Temne trade was further noteworthy in the fifteenth century with the arrival of the Portuguese, and its expansion was evident in the sixteenth century with the arrival of the British and other traders. Slaves, gold, ivory, and local foodstuffs were exchanged for European trade goods, mostly cloth, firearms, and hardware.

I was especially interested in learning about the quickly developing slave trade which ravaged Sierra Leone's people. I found that local traders brought inland slaves to the coast to trade with the Europeans. In the 1700's, many thousands passed through British-run Bunce Island bound mainly for the Americas in South Carolina, Georgia, and North Carolina where my ancestors were enslaved. Sierra Leonean slaves were prized for their skill in rice growing and were especially sought by the slave masters in the markets in the new world.

Informative Conversations with My Sierra Leonean Friends

Centuries after the slave trade ended, I had the opportunity to meet several people whose ancestors came to America from Sierra Leone as slaves. They came to the United States to raise their families and to enjoy the life that is afforded here. However, the horrific wars and the devastating recent Ebola outbreak in Sierra Leone has left the remaining young people with little stability and hope. Therefore, my friends plan to return to Sierra Leone in the future to help with the dire needs of their people, especially the children, and young people.

The following narratives describe my discussions with three of my friends who represent major tribes of Sierra Leone: Mende, Creole, and Temne.

My name is Augusta Fofannti. I am from a town called Pujehum which is located in the southern part of Sierra Leone, West Africa. My late parents used to reside in Freetown which is the Capital of Sierra Leone. I am a member of the Mende tribe, and I speak Mende but also Creole which is the general language of my country. Creole called "broken English" is universally known. Whether educated or not, when you speak Creole you will be understood and can communicate with others.

When I was at home in Sierra Leone, I heard such good things about America. So out of curiosity, I made up my mind to come to America to see this country for myself. And to be honest, I have not been disappointed. America is a beautiful country with a lot of opportunities. If you work hard and play by its rules, "the sky has no limits."

When I came here to live, I decided to go to nursing school to become an LPN (licensed practical nurse). I am now taking classes to become a registered nurse. I have been in the United States for twenty-three years.

Although I love America, after receiving my RN degree, I plan to return to my country and to sign up with the United Nations. It is my desire to work with underdeveloped countries as well as my own. My goal is to train young women to become village or emergency midwives, under the supervision of Registered Nurses. There are so many young women in Sierra Leone and other African countries who need education as well as proper medical care. Unfortunately, Sierra Leone is known for having the highest mortality rate of mothers and newborn babies in the world.

Sierra Leone is a small and beautiful country. It was also a peaceful country until the outbreaks of civil wars caused thousands of innocent people to lose their lives. Mostly young people and children have been severely affected, and they are the target group that I would like to help.

The people of Sierra Leone are a very kind, accommodative, and loving people. We believe that every human being needs to be loved and treated with respect. With open arms and warm hearts, we welcome people from other countries. People of Sierra Leone do not look at other people as strangers, especially black people. You are our brothers and sisters, and we are all Africans; we are one. I am so proud to be of African ancestry. We are a smart and good people. To the author: Thanks for giving me the opportunity to be a part of your book. God bless you.

My name is Jacob August Tarlowoh. I am from Freetown, the Capital of Sierra Leone, West Africa. My people are called Creoles and we speak Krio, which is based mainly on English but also contains elements of West African languages. In the 1700's, my family members were captured as a part of the Atlantic slave trade and taken from Sierra Leone to plantations in South Carolina and Georgia where their rice-farming skills made them especially valuable. In the late 1780's, assisted by Britain, my ancestors, now freed or liberated, returned to Sierra Leone from Cuba, London, Nova Scotia, Jamaica, and other West African countries. Freetown then became one of Britain's first colonies in West Africa.

My family still lives in Sierra Leone on the street where I grew up, so I have fond memories of this community. Our history classes in school always emphasized the determination and resilience of my ancestors in slavery. Although I have found that Africans and African-Americans don't always get the respect that we should in the United States, my ancestors' historic beginnings identify us with the first human civilizations. We also have given extraordinary contributions to the world. This history of my people makes me so proud to be of African ancestry. I am pleased to be from a country whose name means "Lion Roar" which signifies strength and vitality.

I am currently employed as an HVAC Plumber, and God willing, hope to visit Sierra Leone in the near future. I would eventually like to build a home in Sierra Leone and start a plumbing business. It is my desire to train others in my trade. I also would like to further my education while in the United States. I have always been a devout Christian. In Sierra Leone, I worshipped as an Anglican, but currently I am a Presbyterian. In my role as Elder, I serve on the governing body, the Session. I also participate in many church-wide activities.

It is my goal to live a harmonious and healthy lifestyle with my wife, and family. I have a deep and abiding faith in God. Even though there is not much in life that we can control, we must put our trust in God and believe in Him. We must also treat others with respect, kindness, and love.

My name is Jariatu Sama Turay, but my American friends call me Jary.
I am the third of the eleven children of Mr. Yamba Turay and Madam Fatu Sesay. Our family comes from the northern part of Sierra Leone, the Magburaka Tonkolili District.

Though my father did not live long enough to see us grow up, he did leave us with a few stories about the historic slave trade in Sierra Leone. I would like to share one of these stories with you.

This story was told to my father by his great grandfather. It began when three family members were captured just about dinner time. The mother of three young boys saw a group of black and white men coming toward their farm house. The mother screamed to the top of her voice in our Temne language- "Anc potho, Anc Baykya-a, gbukeh nue, Tai nu Teima." Translated it means,

"The white man is coming, run, run don't stop." But it was too late. The three siblings were not able to make it to safety and were captured.

The family members who survived ran into the bush and stayed there for several days. The night of their return to their homes, the Town Crier passed through their village with an important message. He said that the white men who came before did not take the children to harm them. They took the young boys to teach them skills which would benefit them when they returned home from overseas. The boys would be taught how to better cultivate rice, tobacco, and sugar cane. They also would be taught how to make wine and guns to kill the animals that had been destroying their family's farms here in Sierra Leone.

In those days, when a Town Crier came with a message it was usually a communication ordered by the Chief or someone with like authority, so everyone stayed indoors to receive the communication first hand. The Town Crier's message instructed everyone to go to the Community Center the next day to welcome the boys who would be returning home from overseas.

But there was an older family member, Gbenthas Thuray, who could be very troublesome and out-spoken. The meaning of his name was "Verify."

After peeping out of his window and listening to the Town Crier, he thought for a while and then said to the family members who surrounded him, "Tai' nuu Kor dea-a, Annch potho Anc Teh muppnu." Which means "Don't go there, the white man will catch you." When the relatives heard his interpretation, they realized that this was probably a trick, a deceptive plan designed to have them all in one place in order to easily catch and to enslave them. Gbenthas and his relatives also probably understood, which caused them even more concern, that the Chief or others in authority might be the one's responsible for the suspicious trick.

The family then snuck away in the middle of the night and into the thick forest. After a while, they had no food to eat, and sadly realized that they would be unable to keep the chickens and goats that they had brought with them. We know how chickens can start crowing loudly in the morning. The family grew concerned and did not want the crowing chickens to help the slave traders find them. So they decided to quickly eat all the chickens and goats so that there was nothing left to alarm anyone about their location. Later, when they were feeling hungry and facing starvation, they started eating bush animals to survive.

Jary shared additional information with me about the capturing of slaves.

Her father told her that it was the villagers attempt to hide from the slave traders that made it necessary for them to eat bush animals. However, it is also known that some species of bats can carry harmful viruses. One has to wonder if bush meat was the reason for the Ebola outbreak of 2013 which has been traced to a two-year-old child from the village of Gueckedou in south-eastern Guinea, an area where bush meat is frequently hunted and eaten. We know that the Ebola virus did spread from Guinea to other neighboring countries, including Sierra Leone. The Ebola virus severely devastated those countries, causing widespread deaths of families, villages, and crippled their economies.

Another important informational note from Jary regarding slavery speaks to the efforts of village mothers to protect their girls and boys. I have often seen pictures of Africans, boys and men especially, with deeply scarred faces and wondered why their faces were disfigured in this manner? Was it because of a ritual or ceremony which made this necessary? But Jary now gives us an answer. She explains that when the slave traders came and carried the village children and young people away, they took the most attractive and healthy ones. In order to save their offspring from the dreadful experience of a life in slavery, the mothers mutilated their faces to give them an ugly appearance. When the slave traders came they rejected the disfigured children and young people, feeling that they would not sell well in the slave markets. Although disfigured for life, the mothers saved their children and young people from the horror of the middle passage and a life of bondage and slavery in the new world.

A legend of God's intervention on behalf of runaway enslaved women and children

Jary's father then told her that his people truly believed the legend about God's powerful intervention on behalf of runaway slave women and the children they sought to protect. Her father said that there was a place in the Kasseh Chiefdom, part of northern Sierra Leone, where it was believed that a white man could not so much as step there, or he would die instantly. The villagers also believed that a group of mothers and children, seeking a place of refuge, hid in the Kasseh Chiefdom for a long time. It was there that the women led the children in prayer, asking God to cover and to protect them from the white men who could come searching for them and return them to slavery. The mothers stressed in the prayer that the children were orphans and had no parents to help or to provide for them. They later concluded that

God truly answered their prayers and protected them because they were able to live in the bush for many years without any problems. For the villagers, this legend was evidence of God's power to help those who believe and trust in Him and who earnestly pray for His help and assistance. They felt this confirmed that God was unquestionably on the side of the runaway mothers and children rather than the side of the horrible slave traders.

Sierra Leone Elects a Temne as President

It was indeed interesting to learn from *BBC News* that in 2007, Mr. Ernest Bai Koroma was elected Sierra Leones's President. Representing the All Peoples' Congress and his Temne tribe, this former insurance broker won a majority in the parliamentary elections. He accepted the charge and mandate to counter corruption and mismanagement of the state's resources. He also "encouraged foreign investments to repair the damage caused by the civil war."[2]

President Koroma was reelected on November 2012, and his war-torn country gave him 58.7% of the vote. Initially running on a pledge of change, he indicated that he had visibly changed his country's quality of life. Although his opponents voiced serious concerns about the sustainability of his accomplishments, his supporters pointed to newly paved roads and a government health care program which had provided free medical treatment. His opponents also argued that "not enough progress had been made in the decade since the end of the war, drawing attention to Sierra Leone's dismal statistics, which include one of the highest maternal mortality ratings in the world."[3]

The door to our history remains open wide as we learn more and more about our native land through the stories of people who are from Sierra Leone. They have come to our shores as free persons, desiring to benefit from the opportunities now afforded here in America. However, they also share a common history with our ancestors who were brought to these shores against their will and who experienced the horrific trials and sufferings of enslavement.

Endnotes

1. The Temne, "from Israel to Sierra Leone" - Guineelibe
2. BBC News Report, http://www.bbc.com/news/health-29604204
3. Ibid.

Chapter Four
Ghana, Ancestral Birth Place of Our George Family

Newton Othello George and Wife Cecelia Nortey George

What a wonderful surprise and joy when cousin Newton's DNA identified him as a member of the George family from Ghana, their ancestral home. Our roots were now connected to Ghana, a most historic ancient country.

This civilization has played a significant role in the story of humankind. During the colonial period, Ghana was formerly known as the "Gold Coast" because of its abundant gold resources and its enterprising activity in the gold trade.

I have been delighted to learn that Newton's wife, Cecelia, also has Ghanaian roots. It was discovered that Cecelia's father, Andrew Nortey, now deceased, was born of the Ga tribe in Accra, Ghana in a section called Osu Re. Unfortunately, Cecelia had little knowledge of her father because she was raised by an aunt and uncle in Liberia.

Cecelia, who is proud of her multiculturalism, shared that her roots lie both in Ghana and Liberia. Her mother, Claudia Burphy Addison, is of indigenous Liberian and Barbadian decent. An older sister, Ekua, has greatly enriched Cecelia's life by sharing with her their Ghanaian traditions and customs. Cecelia is pleased that Ghana is becoming a country of great modern prominence with a vision toward adding a new chapter to the glorious history and contributions of its ancient people.

Our George Relatives' African Connection: The Fante People of Ghana

Our Fante ancestors (also spelled Fanti) were people of the southern coastal region of Ghana. Most of their history of that time came to us from the revered oral tradition. The Fanti people spoke a dialect called "Akan." Akan is a generic term used to refer to a large number of linguistically related people who live in southern Ghana and the southeastern Cote d'Ivoire (known in English as Ivory Coast). The rise of the early Akan centralized states can be traced to the 13th century and is related to the opening of the trade routes established to move gold throughout the region."[1]

Ghana Came into Prominence as the Empire of Gold

Ghana's name which originally meant "Warrior King," was later replaced to mean "gold." "When the king walked in the capital of Kumbi, he wore a tall golden cap. At his side walked dogs with gold and silver collars. Princes who accompanied the King had strands of gold in their hair."[2]

"Silent Partners" in the Gold and Silver Trade

The rationale behind the methods used by traders in those ancient times demonstrates why the ancient traders were called "silent partners." *Great Empires of West Africa* tells us that "due to a lack of a common language, the exchange of gold and salt took place through silent trade. Not a word was spoken between the traders."[3] We also found that Ghana's location positioned it well for power and success in trade.

In addition to gold, salt was also traded because it was a necessary commodity for health. Like most people living in desert climates, intense sweating caused them to continually lose body fluids which they learned to replace by adding salt to their foods. Salt was also used to preserve foods. This lends credence to a phrase that has been a part of my life and culture: "Salt is worth its weight in gold."

The traders exercised great care and precision as they, in silence, bought and sold their salt and gold. Research reveals "that the salt traders left their blocks of salt on the ground at some distance from the gold traders and then retreated a little way. The gold traders then approached to examine the amount of salt. After leaving what they felt was a fair amount of gold in payment for the salt, they, too, withdrew. The salt traders came back to examine the amount of gold. If they accepted it, the transaction was complete. If they did not, the process was repeated until agreement was reached."[3]

This brief glimpse into the history and customs of our Ghanaian ancestors confirms Ghana as one of the earliest civilizations of humankind that advanced to become a great empire. Their exemplary leadership made them powerful traders of gold in ancient times.

My Role as Godmother Opens the Door to Ghana's Ancient Traditions

On March 8, 1992, I was called to serve as Minister of Evangelism for a church in Maryland. This small, white congregation, located in a changing community, was now challenged to open its doors to new multinational neighbors. My role, as an ethnic minority minister, was to design programs that would welcome our new neighbors and introduce them to our church's worship and activities. Many of the persons moving into our community were from African and Spanish speaking countries, as well as the Caribbean.

New community residents were very responsive to our warm welcome and outreach. Some visited to learn more about us, while others joined as new members and soon became an integral part of the church's fellowship. Creative programs were instituted such as: International Nights where native dress was worn and ethnic dishes savored; Bible Study in Minister's Homes for small group interaction, discussion, and learning; Small Group Meetings in Parishioners' Homes where an ethnic dinner and faith stories could be shared.

The church became such a cohesive faith community that some of the traditions of our new membership began to influence our relationship with one another. African new born babies were named for white members, and I became Godmother for four parishioners. My husband, Albert, an avid sportsman and athlete, was expected and delighted to attend many of the teenagers' sports events. Also, Robert Finzel, who earlier had been one of the host members, was now Albert's best buddy. For years Robert, fondly called Bob, and Albert were regular attendees at nearby University of Maryland's sports events. This activity ended only when the two buddies could no longer get up and down the stadium's bleachers because of their advancing years. Oh, how Albert and Bob looked forward not only to the games but the hot dogs, which neither of them was supposed to eat.

I gained four goddaughters in my new role; Veda and Vida are African and Tasha and Geraldine are African-American. I will focus on Vida who is from Ghana, our family's ancestral homeland.

I found the role and responsibilities of Godmother in the Ghanaian tradition to be similar to the practices of my African-American family and community. This similarity confirms that many of our traditions handed down from our African ancestors are practiced today. We both envisioned Godmother to be that guiding, caring, and protecting person who would be an active participant in a godchild's growth and development. A Godmother would also be expected to step up and fully assume the "mother role," if something happened to the natural mother. A Godmother also had a role in the godchild's spiritual and religious development.

I was really surprised when Vida approached me with a request to be her Godmother. She shared that she was now engaged to marry Percy who was also a new member. They were beginning to make wedding plans. Vida further indicated that her mother would soon leave the United States to live permanently in Ghana. This is why she and her mother discussed asking me to accept the role of Godmother and to be their family's representative here in America.

Although Vida and Percy planned to be married in Maryland, the couple also desired to have a traditional ceremony and celebration in Ghana. Vida then indicated her hope that my husband, Albert, and I, in addition to becoming her Godparents, would travel to Ghana with them. She really wanted us to experience and participate in a traditional Ghanaian marriage with its elaborate ceremony and gala celebrations.

The day of their initial marriage arrived and there was much excitement as we met at the court for the ceremony which was performed by a justice of the peace. Below is the picture of the happy couple on their wedding day.

Vida and Percy Agyei-Obese

A Gift Befitting a Ghanaian King and Queen

Unfortunately, I became ill, and Albert and I had to give up our plan to attend the wedding in Ghana. Vida and Percy came to visit just before leaving for their grand celebration and promised to tell us every detail when they returned. Later, the stories they shared were so vivid that we felt we had actually experienced the celebrations with them.

We were also pleasantly surprised by a set of matching Ghanaian outfits that they brought for both of us. The outfits made us feel that we were really an ancient Ghanaian King and Queen. (See pictured below)

The Godparents in their New Outfits, Attending a Kwanzaa Celebration

Our Cousin Cecelia Introduces Us to Her Own Ghanaian Salad

Pictured: Cousin Newton complimenting Cecelia for being a wonderful wife, mother, and an outstanding Ghanaian cook.

Recipe for Cecelia's Ghanaian Salad

One whole Rotisserie Chicken (pulled away from bones in small long pieces)
4-5 boiled eggs (sliced)
4 tomatoes sliced or diced

Recipe for Cecelia's Ghanaian Salad (continued)

1 small red onion sliced thinly
2 yellow peppers sliced in thin strips or diced
2 red peppers sliced in thin strips or diced
2 bags of Dole Classic Romaine mix (9 oz. bag)
1 bunch of spinach
1 (14.9 oz.) bottle Heinz Salad Cream (only sold at African Produce Store/Market)
1 can of Heinz beans (approximately 14 oz.) from African Market
Sea salt and ground black pepper

You need to have most of the ingredients in separate bowls before mixing them. All the peppers and onions can be together in one bowl.

This is a large layered salad. It feeds about 15 persons. Put in handfuls of lettuce mix, sprinkle tomatoes, a bit of red onions, a few beans, a little of the colored peppers, very tiny sprinkle of salt, a handful spinach, pieces of sliced eggs, and pieces of chicken, then drizzle with the salad cream. Repeat (continue layering) the same ingredients until you run out of ingredients. Only put the ground black pepper on the second layer. Each time drizzling enough salad cream over each layer. You will need to use the entire bottle (14.9 oz.). This salad is a meal by itself.

It gets soggy if not eaten in a day. When it gets soggy, just add more lettuce. It also shrinks while transporting. In the summer, it gets soggy fast but since it has no mayonnaise and the chicken is fully cooked, it can be left unrefrigerated all day.

The Ghanaian Kitchen and Role of the Housewife

A friend, Bertha Martin, and I were talking about my book and this chapter. She indicated that she has traveled to Ghana several times and has a friend there who has written a cook book entitled, *The Art of West African Cooking*. I was really intrigued, and when she later gave me the book to read, I concluded that the author, Dinah Ameley Ayensu's, narrative about the housewife was worth sharing with you.

The following snippets from Dinah Ayensu's Introduction will tell us about some of the activity in the Ghanaian kitchen, and the housewife who reigns supreme in that arena.

Dinah shares that the kitchen is traditionally an active meeting place for women who not only talk about foods, but also use this as an opportunity to gossip as well.

The housewife is the main cook and she plays an important, dominant, and responsible role. Her day could start as early as 4:30 a.m. Every day she shops at the market for fresh fruits and vegetables. But most importantly, it is the custom to stop along the way to market to visit briefly with friends and to inquire about their health.

The author tells us that the method used for adding ingredients can vary from dish to dish, but the sequence is very important. She explains: "Onion, pepper, tomatoes, and salt are always added sequentially for some specific dishes. If a specific sequence is not followed, a sight change in appearance and taste of the dish will result and the cook may be called to task.[4]

It is also customary to have young, female family members present in the kitchen to assist the housewife. The goal is to teach the young girls to cook like their mothers by the time they reach marriage age. The following are some of the steps they are taught to master:

> 1) How to add condiments to stews and soups.
> 2) How to prepare such basic meals as peanut butter soup, meat or fish stew, and boiled vegetables."[5]

All young women are expected to know how to cook by the time they are married. They surely would be an embarrassment to the bride's parents if she is found to be a bad cook. The West African housewife does not usually use a cookbook. Until recently, it was considered disgraceful to use one. Therefore, even the best cooks did not write their recipes down. Instead they were passed down verbally to their children.

I do hope that this brief discussion of the Ghanaian Kitchen and the role of the housewife will invite you to seek more information about the traditions and customs of our people with whom we share an ancestral heritage. I also hope that your observation of just how pleased our Cousin Newton was with Cousin Cecelia's cooking will inspire you to use her recipe and savor her wonderful salad. Remember all you young ladies, it is said that "The way to a man's heart is through his stomach." So take notice and enjoy.

Final Word

In this chapter and in Chapter Three, it has been the author's desire to help our family members and readers view our ancestral past though the voices and stories of people who are from our ancestral countries. The slave traders, slave holders, and masters carefully and systemically stripped all connection to the original homelands from our ancestor's memory banks. They were therefore unaware of their heritage and connection to an outstanding history, one that spoke to the contributions of a noble people who extended back to the beginning of time. Even though our enslavers used our skills and abilities to build the great nations of our time, they also told our ancestors that they were inferior beings who should not be recognized as human. Unfortunately, that message still resonates today. It is against this back drop that I have devoted this chapter to a short synopsis of the history, traditions, customs, and delicious cuisines of Ghana, our ancestral birthplace.

Endnotes

1. Fante- Art 7 Life in Africa – The University of Iowa Museum of Art
http://Africa.uima.uiowa.edu/peoples/show/Fante
2. Chapter Two, Great Empires of West Africa (500 -1600), 16. The African American Experience/ a history, the globe book company
3. Ibid., xiv
4. Ibid., 17, 18
5. *The Art of West African Cooking*, Dinah Ameley Ayensu, 1994, Introduction III

Chapter Five
The Tie that Binds

"We are each other's harvest; we are each other's business; we are each other's magnitude and bond."

-Gwendolyn Brooks

Our African Ancestors greatly impacted American life with the skills and talents brought from the Ancient civilizations of Africa. Despite their horrific enslavement, and their captor's efforts to erase their former lives from memory, they were able to integrate these gifts and talents into the fabric of American society and culture.

It has been surprising to me that scholars have debated whether our ancestors were able to bring former life skills into their new world experience. Indeed, this was the reason for the Transatlantic Slave Trade—the demonic plot and strategy that preyed upon our ancestors. Our kin folks were equipped with knowledge and abilities that our captives did not possess. The Euro-American captives realized their limitations and saw our ancestors as a viable source of knowledge, skills, and currency to create a New World Order. This would be an unending source of free labor, because it was a life sentence for our African ancestors. Freedom would always be denied; death was the only release.

One of the immediate contributions which shaped American life was African traditional cooking. Research tells us that, upon the slave ships, during the middle passage, African women were the ones responsible for the cooking of meals. The women, therefore, cooked their traditional African foods and attempted to continue this practice when they finally arrived at the farms and plantations where they were enslaved. An article from National Geographic News further tells us, "When our enslaved ancestors had the opportunity they began to plant the seeds of the traditional foods they were forced to leave behind."[1]

The African and slavery traditions that our cousins brought to their new lives in Liberia, Africa.

Our African Ancestors were brought to the American colonies against their will and in shackles. Now their kin folks find themselves faced with an opportunity to leave this country that has also degraded, held them hostage, and made real freedom an elusive objective. Going to Liberia with the Marcus Garvey Movement, in the 1920's, however, would have its own unknowns. But our family would now step out on faith feeling that any move would be better than remaining in the American colonies.

Telling this story through my conversations with Mama Jessie, will offer an understanding of the dynamics that we each carry to our new experiences. We usually struggle to hold on to things that define who we are. Innately we tend to hold on to objects and traditions which offer us a sense of security, nurture, and comfort—providing a support system for survival in unknown circumstances. When my cousin Jestina Gibson, lovingly referred by me as Mama Jessie, and I met for the first time, we brought many questions to the fore. These questions held the potential to confirm our relationship as cousins and answers that could shed light on traditions that we practice but often wonder how they began. There were also questions about the traits that we exhibit—what are their origins?

We were so happy, to have this opportunity, and could barely wait for an answer to be completed, in order to ask the next question. Mama Jessie excitedly asked, "Are there twins in your family? No one in our Liberian George family has twins but me." I quickly confirmed that I have heard that, my Grandmother Rhoda and Grandfather Edward Dudley George, had a set of twins, in their family of sixteen children. I also added, that my father was a surviving twin and his daughter Alma had Billy and Johnnie, who are identical twins. This also raises on two accounts, the possibility that my grandchildren and beyond could have twins. Mama Jessie, who is an accomplished seamstress, then asked, "Do any of you have short arms." I was amused by the question, and replied, "I have short arms and always have my sleeves cut to accommodate my arm length." We gleefully hugged each other, feeling this really affirmed that we are related, and are cousins.

My question to Mama Jessie was in relation to foods. She immediately told me that her family's diet includes both American and foods of the Liberian indigenous tradition. As we compared how we both prepare our foods, we were amazed that we each prepare them in the same manner. These similarities also reflect the traditions of our enslaved fore-parents. Jestina then recalled, with fond memories, the family gatherings in Caldwell, when a pig was cooked in a hole [earth or pit]. She remembered her grandmother oiling the pig and then sifting herbs over it, "What a pleasant aroma that made, as the pig cooked on the fires below it!" I, too, had memories of visiting Cousin Rosalie's family home in North Carolina, when the men gathered before day-break and prepared the pig for roasting above the pit, where hot coals were placed. After a slow roasting, the pig was ready for our picnic feast by noontime, when everyone gathered. We both laughed at the many ways we ate the pig: pig feet, pig ears, and salt pork to season collards, cabbage and other greens. We also made corn bread, corn pone, rum and pound cake with the same recipes. We were tickled and pleased to see that we make potato salad with some of the same ingredients: onions, pickles, sometimes eggs, and mayonnaise—this was the base with other seasonings added, such as celery, a dash of mustard, topped with paprika.

Our Liberian cousins held on to the African-American tradition of visiting one another after work or on weekends. There was always extra food at meal time or something special to share with relatives who might stop by. And for both our families that custom remains today. One of the most important traditions that our families observed was to cook "Hoppin' John" on New Year's Day. This was a black–eyed peas and rice dish. There is a saying: "Eat poor that day. Eat rich the rest of the year." Our families feel that this traditional dish will bring good luck and prosperity for the New Year.

Karen Pinchin, writer for the National Geographic, tells us:

> "This red pea, which originated in Africa and is the original ingredient in the region's quintessential rice and beans dish Hoppin' John, is just one of the many heritage crops from the African Continent receiving new attention from farmers, chefs, scientists, and food historians. Growing numbers of researchers, many of them African–American, are bringing to light the uncredited ways the slaves and their descendants have shaped how Americans eat...Slave owners sent back and got seeds for what the slaves were used to eating, because they weren't used to the food here in America. "That meant the slaves could plant for themselves," said Bailey (Cornelia Walker Bailey who grew up in Sapelo Island Georgia.) Bailey says her favorite way to eat the peas is in a traditional dish with stewed meat and okra, another plant that originated in Africa. "I had quite a few okra dishes when I went to West Africa. They had it in stews and stuff—very, very similar to what we eat here," she says. The

strange dishes they were serving us weren't strange to me, because I was going, 'Hey, we eat this back home.'"[2]

My conversations with Mama Jessie and Jestina has given me a glimpse of their family's life in Liberia and we can see how much we have in common. Not only do we have similar physical characteristics but we celebrate, observe like customs, and prepare many food items in the same manner.

But so important to our beginning premise, in this chapter, we can conclude that our enslaved ancestors did bring to this New World traditions and talents which are a vital part of our society and nation. Our families have held fast to these attributes, handed down from our enslaved kinfolks, whose contributions and legacy provides us with a pathway for survival and a model for constructive living. Our ancestors, despite their horrific enslavement—did not give up. They continued to persevere, yearned, and prayed for freedom. We now stand on our ancestor's shoulders and it is because of them that we can now share our gifts and talents and contributions in the communities where we live.

Skills brought to the New World by enslaved African ancestors.

Our African ancestors, though enslaved and receiving horrific treatment, impacted American life with skills utilized in their Motherland, Africa. My research and in particular the work of Joseph E. Holloway, author of *African Contributions to American Culture*, confirm this.

"Africans, and their descendants, contributed to the richness and fullness of American culture from its beginnings. Their contributions in early America for which they have received little or no credit, include the development of the American dairy industry, open grazing of cattle, artificial insemination of cows, the development of vaccines (including vaccination for smallpox), and cures for snake bites."

"African stories and folklore, such as the Brer Rabbit, Brer Fox, and Chicken Little tales originated in Africa and were absorbed into America's culture of childhood and laid a foundation for American nursery culture. Despite the limitations imposed by slavery, Africans and their descendants made substantial contributions to American culture in aesthetics, animal husbandry, agriculture, cuisine, folklore, folk medicine, and language"

It is clear that early Africans brought with them highly developed skills, which were in turn used to also develop the architecture and goods sold in town— "laboring in metal, iron, leather, pottery, and weaving. Senegambians were employed as medicine men [root doctors], blacksmiths, harness makers, carpenters, and lumberjacks. These trades were passed down to other enslaved Africans by the skilled African craftsmen in an apprentice-type fashion."[3]

Our Ancestors helped Introduce Rice to the New World.

Reading the work of Joseph A. Opala, *The Gullah: Rice, slaves, and the Sierra Leone – America Connection*, raises the possibility that my Bryant relatives helped introduce rice to the colonies. Our DNA identifies Sierra Leone as our country of origin. Because rice brought great profit to our captives, South Carolina became rich and prosperous. Rice agriculture has been called "the best opportunity for industrial profit which 18th century America afforded. In this way South Carolina became one of the richest of the North American colonists."[4]

The South Carolina planters were initially ignorant of rice cultivation and their experiments in this specialty failed. However, they began to recognize that it could be advantageous to import slaves from West Africa, a traditional rice producing region. These slaves already had the technical knowledge and skills of rice production. Also it was determined that South Carolina was about the same size as Sierra Leone and had similar geography and climate. The South Carolina rice planters were willing to pay higher prices for slaves from the "Rice Coast," the "Windward Coast," the "Gambia," and "Sierra – Leone" ...When slave traders arrived in Charleston with slaves from the rice-growing region, they were careful to advertise their origin on auction posters or in newspaper announcements, sometimes noting that the slaves were accustomed to the planting of rice.[5]

The South Carolina and Georgia colonists were able to finalize a system of rice cultivation that depended on the labor patterns, technical skills, and knowledge brought by their African slaves. Our enslaved ancestors also possibly contributed to a variety of irrigation systems used on those rice plantations.

During the growing season the slaves on the rice plantations moved through the fields in a line, hoeing rhythmically and singing work songs to keep in union. At harvest time the women processed the rice by pounding it in large wooden mortars and pestles, virtually identical to those used in West Africa, and then "fanning" the rice in large round winnowing baskets to separate the grain and chaff. The slaves may also have contributed to the system of "sluices,"[6.] banks, and ditches 'used on the South Carolina and Georgia rice plantations.

Our DNA exploration tells us that our Bryant ancestors are from Sierra Leone and spoke the "Temne" language. Opala, in his research, raises, for us, the possibility that our enslaved Bryant relatives could also have been imported to South Carolina [as well as North Carolina] and therefore, greatly contributed to the rice production and irrigation systems of South Carolina and Georgia.

Travelers in the 1700s noted that West African farmers—including the Temne of Sierra Leone ---were constructing elaborate irrigations systems for rice cultivation. In South Carolina and Georgia, the slaves simply continued with many of the methods of rice farming to which they were accustomed in Africa.[7]

Our Enslaved African's Story and Contribution to the Cowboy Culture

Often the contributions and stories of enslaved Africans have been embraced by our captives as their own and our roles not talked about or entered into history books. The contributions and stories of the Black cowboy is an example of this. Even though our family's history does not have a direct connection to the cowboy culture we must, at every opportunity, tell the stories of our "Universal" African family.

So now we lift up the Fulani people from Senegambia and will tell of the skills and knowledge they brought from our motherland which then impacted the cowboy culture of this new world, even until today.

Enslaved African-Americans brought from their homelands in Africa, knowledge, innovations, and many skills in cattle raising, animal husbandry, open grazing patterns, and cattle drives. These contributions greatly impacted American colonial life. The work of Holloway confirms this in the following excerpts cited from his research:

> The first major contribution by Africans to North American society was in the area of cattle raising. When the Fulani (or Fula) people from Senegambia along with Longhorn cattle, were imported to South Carolina in 1731, colonial herds increased from 500 to 6,784 some 30 years later.
>
> These Fulas were expert cattlemen and were responsible for introducing African husbandry patterns of open grazing now practiced throughout the American cattle industry. Cattle drives to the centers of distribution were innovations Africans brought with them as contributions to a developing industry.
>
> Originally a *cowboy* was an African who worked with cattle, just as a houseboy worked in "de big House." Open grazing made practical use of an abundance of land and a limited labor force.
>
> Africans and their descendants were America's first cowboys. Most people are not aware that many cowboys of the American West were [Black], contrary to how the film industry and the media have portrayed them. Only recently have we begun to recognize the extent to which cowboy culture has African roots. Many details of cowboy life, work, and even material culture can be traced to the Fulani, America's first cowboys, but there has been little investigation of this by historians of the American West.

Enslaved Africans, despite the obstruction and subjugation by the white ruling class, were able to bring their African architecture, with its history and culture, to the New World.

> Africa is a sizable continent with a multitude of cultural traditions. The sub total of native African architecture is derived from indigenous African empires and states, and from imported European, Midwestern and Asian societies. The architecture is influenced by Moorish invasions, Egyptian pharaohs and all they engendered, nomadic foragers, hunter-gatherers, stable agricultural societies,

desert dwellers, and ongoing tribal identities and conflicts, diverse religions, witchcraft and more.[8]

Holloway shows us why and how the White slave owners controlled all Architectural efforts by African Americans.

When one views African traits in American architecture before and after slavery, it becomes clear that the focus must be on special sensitivities. In terms of materials, techniques, and design, severe limits were placed on African American architects.

Both the plantation owners and non-owners alike saw architecture as a way of controlling one's life and destiny, through similarity, reinforcing the memory of a homeland and a sense of security in a hostile environment. Thus, [they felt] as soon as the control of the built environment passed to the African, the Europeans' position and sense of authority, control, and power were threatened. The slave artisan was therefore denied the power of self-expression through architecture.

"According to Dagon philosophy, the house serves as a womb and a cradle from where culture is learned. It represents an image of a community and expresses a group's social universe. The power which culture depends upon is derived from the house, and a cultural identity and personality can be understood by the concept of it."

The all-Black Towns movement was an effort by African Americans to fight back against the control and segregation imposed by the racist society that ruled them.

As a response to the atrocities of a violent hostile racist society, the advocates of self-segregation saw all-Black towns as an important step toward security. The all-Black town ideology sought to combine economic self-help and moral uplift with racial pride. The all-Black town's movement came from the realization that the American "melting pot" only melted for those of European heritage.

In response to American racism numerous Black towns grew. They included: Nicodemus, Kansas (1879); Mound Bayou, Mississippi (1887); Langston City, Oklahoma (1891);

Clear view, Oklahoma (1903); Boley, Oklahoma (1904); Backdom, New Mexico; Hobson City, Alabama; Allensworth, California, and Rentiesville, Oklahoma.

Archeological investigation of Black townships and sizes, materials and relative proximity of houses, the hierarchy of building placement, and a variety of artifacts, found clear evidence of African origin. It shows how an African design has remained paramount in the Black architectural experience in America.[9]

Our reference details some Architectural skills that were brought to this New World by enslaved African artisans.

Africans brought with them to the New World the ability to use wood, metal, earth and stone. Their ability to adapt indigenous materials made them indispensable as workers for Euro-Americans.

A prime example of a disguised or unrecognized African architectural influence is the porch. A common feature in many areas of West and Central Africa, the porch is an African contribution to American architecture as a whole.

Pierce Lewis wrote: "It was long before Southerners could bring themselves to attach porches to their Georgina Town Houses. Albert Simmons indicates that porches did not become common until after the 1790s, when refugees from Haiti arrived in Charleston...It is not inconceivable that millions of enslaved Africans, upon who Euro-Americans were dependent, taught their masters more about tropical architecture than they are willing to acknowledge.

On the Sea Island coast of Georgia, enslaved Africans developed a building material called *tabby*, a burnt lime and seashell aggregate used prolifically as building materials for walls, fences and roadways... The Brick Street Baptist Church foundation was constructed out of this tabby material as well as the graveyard head stones in the graves of the Penn Center, to the Slave hospital at the Retreat Plantation on St. Simons Island, Georgia.

The slave quarters of Keswick, near Midlothian, Virginia were constructed around 1750 and made with the African tradition of hand –made burnt clay bricks by plantation slaves. The slave quarters are reminiscent of the circular structures of Kasai Province in Zaire.

Thomas Day, a cabinetmaker and architectural interior woodwork designer from Milton, North Carolina, was the fifth wealthiest man in the country according to the 1850 federal census record.

Although servicing an exclusively white clientele, he was able to create African-influenced products. Using carving techniques that required "set-in" elements and an anthropological ordering of scale, he was able to reflect the African tradition of the Bakongo of Zaire.

African American architects attempted to incorporate African architectural designs into the plantations and many buildings they built, thus creating an African presence. African American buildings and early structures were transmitters of this culture. They transmitted the culture of the past into the living present, which served as monuments for the future.[10]

The Influence of African Dance on America's Dance Culture

Deep in the hearts and minds of every Ancestral enslaved person was the desire for freedom and the dance was the perfect release for the pent up emotions they experienced. Dance was reminiscent of the African homeland where that release was often depicted as joy, celebration, ritual, and worship. Now dance was the expression of their suppressive agony and a desire for freedom, to live a good life, no longer under the rule of their captives. Dance often created for the master's enjoyment evolved into forms that represented their previous African cultures. Holloway now confirms this for us:

The dance now known as the Charleston had the greatest influence on American dance culture than any other imported African dance. It is a form of the jitterbug dance, which is a general term applied too unconventional, often formless and energetic social dances performed to syncopated music. Enslaved Africans brought it from the Kongo to Charleston, South Carolina, as the juba dance, which then slowly evolved into what is now the Charleston. (Kongo-became Congo).

> This [the Charleston] one-legged sembuka step, over-and-cross, arrived in Charleston between 1735 and 1740. Similar

in type to the "one-legged" sembuka-style dancing found in northern Kongo, the dance consists of "patting" (otherwise known as "patting Juba"), stamping, clapping, and slapping of arms, chest, and so forth.

The name "Charleston" was given to the Juba dance by European Americans. In Africa, however, the dance is called the Juba or Djouba.

Enslaved Africans maintained their music, song, and dance cultures as they adapted to life in the New World. Many African dances survived because they were reshaped and adopted by European Americans, while others remained intact or changed with the new circumstances. For example, the ring shout started as a sacred Kongolese dance, but later found expression in non-sacred forms of dance.

In both Africa and the New World, the circle ritual had different meanings in the distinct cultures. In the Kongo, the ring shout circle is identical to the Gullah counterclockwise dance, which is linked to the most important African ceremony – the rites of passage. Among the Mande, the circle dance is a part of the marriage and birth ceremonies, and in Wolof culture, the ring circle is central to most dancing.[11]

African Musical Instrument's Connection to New World Music

The African banjo was first made known through our ancestors in southern slave communities. It has also been acknowledged that the banjo was brought to the new colonies through the middle passage experience. The original banjo then made some evolutionary changes as Anglo- American influences were introduced. A site for educational purposes entitled, *US Slave: The American Banjo and American music* tells us about the banjo's history and evolution.

First introduced to the United States by African Americans in southern slave communities, the early banjo was construed with a gourd head and four gut or vine strings. Early, relatively primitive designs of the instrument are African in origin and modern (designs) vaguely resemble these early versions. The banjo was introduced to Anglo-American culture in the early nineteenth century.

Banjos belong to a family of instruments that are very old. Drums with strings stretched over them can be traced throughout the Far East, the Middle East and Africa from the beginning. They can be played like the banjo, bowed or plucked like a harp depending on their environment. These instruments were spread, in "modern" times, to Europe through the Arab conquest of Spain, and the Ottoman conquest of the Balkans. The banjo, as we can begin to recognize it, was made by African slaves based on instruments that were indigenous to their parts of Africa. These early "banjos" were spread to the colonies of those countries engaged in the slave trade.

Scholars have found that many of these instruments have names that are related to the modern word "banjo", such as "banjil", "Banza", "bangoe", "Bangie", "banshaw". Some historians mention the diaries of Richard Johnson as the first record of the instrument... While exploring the Gambra River in Africa in 1620 he recorded an instrument" ...made of a great gourd and a neck, thereunto was fastened strings. The first mention of the name for these instruments in the Western Hemisphere is from Martinique in a document dated 1678. It mentions slave gatherings where an instrument called the "banza" is used.... The best known is probably that of Thomas Jefferson in 1781: "The instrument proper to them (i.e. the slaves) is the Banjar, which they brought hither from Africa."[12]

Our Own African American Family Artisan, Mr. Black, Is Remembered and Celebrated

Mr. George Henry Black and President Richard Milhous Nixon. President Nixon was the 37th President of the United States and served (1969 – 1974)

I can remember, my son, Gerald, excitedly calling me, to tell me that his great grandfather has been invited to the White House, to be commissioned by President Nixon as a State Department diplomat. Mr. George Henry Black, a 92-year-old artisan, was being recognized for his ability to make bricks, an art form, that has brought him great accolades in his home town of Winston Salem, North Carolina. He would now travel to Guyana and share his craft with the villagers there.

His wonderful story can be found in "A Life on the Road", Chapter 17, by Charles Kuralt, published by G.P. Putman & Sons, 1990. Charles Kuralt was an award winning broadcast journalist with CBS Evening News. For more than 30 years Mr. Kuralt was the host of the CBS News' "Sunday Morning."

We will now learn how Mr. Black ascended to Presidential recognition, as told by the Journalist, Mr. Charles Kuralt.

George Black was a brick maker. He turned out to be a pretty good diplomat for the State Department too, but that part of the story comes later. George Black was a brick maker, the craft he and his brother chose when their father died in 1889.

"We aren't going to get to go to school," his brother fourteen, said to George, eleven. "We're going to have to work for a living. If we haul ourselves up and make men out of ourselves, even if we don't know A from B, we'll make somebody call us 'Mr. Black' someday."

Mr. Black quoted his brother with pride more than eighty years later. He was a tall dignified man. Everybody called him, Mr. Black.

The little boys, George and his brother, setting out on their own in 1889, walked the forty miles from Randleman, North Carolina to Winston-Salem. They apprenticed themselves to a brick maker for a while and, after they learned the trade, they started their own business while they were still in their teens. Since well before the turn of the century, George Black had been making bricks the way I watched him do it one afternoon in his backyard.

He had a mule hitched to what he called a "mud mill." With his giant practiced hands, Mr. Black scooped up the mud mixed by the paddles of the mill as the mule plodded in a circle, and packed the mud expertly into six-brick forms ready for the kiln.

"How many bricks do you figure you've made in your life?" I asked him.

"O Lord." He said. "I don't know. I'd be most afraid to know." He handed a finished form to one of the neighborhood youngsters who were serving as stackers that day and impatiently awaited another stack of empties.

"I made a million bricks in one year," he said. "Mr. R J. Reynolds rode out here on a white horse. He always rode a white horse, you know. He asked me if I thought I could make a thousand bricks. He said he had in mind to build a tobacco factory. I studied and said yes, I could. I did, too, and you can go downtown and see them if you want to. That building is still there. They're all my bricks. Yes, Sir."

I found myself filled with admiration for this man standing in a pit before me in mud up to his elbows. He had made a life of the basic elements, water and earth and fire. And he had made the building blocks of a city.

Mr. Black dressed up in his Sunday suit the next day and took me on a stroll about Winston–Salem.

"These blocks we've been walking on," he said, as we passed through the restored village of Old Salem, I made these only about forty years ago. They're holding up nice. Yeah."

He pointed with his cane. "I made the bricks for the building over there." It was a schoolhouse. "I made the bricks for the Old Home Church over there." He said. "I made the bricks for that brick wall yonder." Wherever we walked, he pointed out the work of his own hands.

When we reached the block – long R.J Reynolds factory, he said. "I believe I told you wrong about this job. It wasn't a million bricks. It ended up being a million and a half." He leaned on his walking stick and looked up at the massive structure. "Made these bricks six at a time," he said. "Put 'em out on the board and put 'em in a kiln and burned 'em for a dollar and a half a day. You don't know it but that was good pay in those days. Yes, sir."

We walked on. "Made all these bricks six at a time." Mr. Black said, "and I'm going to make some more yet!"

The morning after our story about Mr. Black went on the air, I was sitting on the edge of my bed in a motel room, rubbing my eyes and trying to figure out where to go next, when the phone rang. It was the CBS News State Department Correspondent at the time, Marvin Kalb.

He said, "There's a guy here at the Agency for International Development who wants to talk with you. His name is Harvey J. Witherell. He's on the Guyana desk over there. I think he probably is the Guyana desk. I don't know what he wants with you, but he has been calling me all morning. I wish you'd give him a ring and get him off my neck."

"Sure Marvin," I said.

"If it turns out to be anything I can help you with, let me know." Marvin said generously, and a little wearily. The life of a State Department correspondent must be hard. He has the whole world to worry about all the time.

When I reached Harvey J. Witherell, his voice was trembling with excitement.

"I hear you had a story about a brick maker on television last night," he said.

"Yep," I said.

"Oh, gosh, I've been looking all over the country for a brick maker who still does the job by hand." Harvey J. Witherell said. I didn't think there were any left. What's he like."

"He's a nice man," I said.

"You see, Harvey J. Witherell said, "the government of Guyana wants us to send a brick maker down there. They have a Five Year Plan or something like that to rebuild the whole country in brick. There's no shortage of raw materials. I mean there's plenty of mud in Guyana, but they don't want to build a big brick factory. They want somebody to go village-to-village for a couple of weeks to teach people how to make bricks for themselves."

"Well," I said, "I've got just the man for you, Harvey, but he is ninety-two years old."

"I don't care how old he is, "Harvey said. "I think he's the last brick maker." I gave him Mr. Black's address and telephone number. "You have made my day!" said Harvey J. Witherell.

Mr. Black's Contract with Guyana

The very next day, on official government business and carrying his government briefcase, Harvey I. Witherell caught a plane from Washington to Winston - Salem. He and Mr. Black hit it off. They came to an agreement that amounted to one of the best deals in the history of American foreign aid. Mr. Black would go to Guyana for 10 days. He would take his granddaughter, Evelyn Abrams, who also knew how to make bricks, and a kid from the neighborhood, Thomas Brabham, and they would go down there and teach those people how to make bricks. Mr. Black would be paid $100.00 per day. Not much. I thought when I heard about it, but better than the dollar and a half he got from R.J. Reynolds.

An unfortunate development cancelled Mr. Henry J. Witherell's Dream for Mr. Black.

Some High official of the agency for International Development, some administrator whose job it was to review agency proposals and give them final approval, some insensible overseer, reading one of the forms Harvey Witherell had prepared in triplicate describing Mr. Black and the perfect match of the man to the mission, said to himself, wait a minute, this man is *ninety-two years old*! He reached for a stamp, one that said "Cancelled," or perhaps "DENIED," stamped all over the proposal, and sent it tumbling back down through the Bureaucracy, where it landed with a thud on the desk of Harvey J. Witherell.

The Wheels of the News Media Brought a Different Result

There was a good newspaper in Winston-Salem, the *Sentinel*. Somebody on the newspaper heard about Mr. Black's forthcoming trip and said, "That's a pretty good story." The Sentinel ran the story on page one: "Mr. Black is going to Guyana."

The people at the United Press wire service read the Winston- Salem *Sentinel*. Somebody there said: "That's a pretty good story. The UPI picked up the story and transmitted it nationwide: "Mr. Black is going to Guyana."

The Washington Post subscribes to the United Press wire service. Some editor there said, "That's a pretty good story." *The Washington Post* printed it with a Wire photo of Mr. Black and his mud mill: "Mr. Black is going to Guyana."

The White House reads *The Washington Post*. Somebody at the White House said, "That's a pretty good story," and showed it to somebody else, who said, "Wouldn't it be wonderful if the President would see this man off?"

The timing could not have been more perfect. On precisely the day Mr. Black's trip to Guyana was being cancelled by the State Department, the White House was inviting Mr. Black to stop off in Washington on his way to Guyana for the State Department, to meet the President in the Oval Office.

Harvey J. Witherell, sitting there amid the wreckage of his dream, let his eye fall on the President's appointment schedule for the next week as published in the Official Register.

"10A.M. Wednesday," one item read. "George Black, brick maker of Winston-Salem, N.C., who is going to Guyana to teach brickmaking at the invitation of U.S. AID."

"This made Harvey J. Witherell feel much better. Whistling a little tune, he tore this item, highlighting it with a yellow marker, and confidently sent back up the bureaucracy to the official who had marked his idea "Cancelled".

Of course all the wheels that hours before had rolled backward to a halt now started running fast forward again.

The project just stamped "Cancelled" was stamped "High Priority."

Mr. Black meets President Nixon and then goes to Guyana to fulfill his mission to teach brickmaking to the villagers.

So George Black got to meet the President and so did his close relatives. He did go to Guyana. I [Mr. Charles Kuralt] went along. There, Mr. Black taught brickmaking with such energy that he exhausted his official hosts, his village pupils, and a retinue of U.S. Government hirelings, one of whom was probably the very official who had told Harvey J. Witherell that Mr. Black was too old for this trip.

One day, Mrs. Forbes Burnham, wife of the Prime Minister, fashionably dressed in a riding outfit, came out to one of the villages in a limousine to be photographed for the local press with the visiting American brick maker. Mr. Black nodded to her, extended a muddy hand, and went back to teaching brickmaking.

"He is quite a man," Mrs. Burnham said, as someone came up with a towel to wipe the mud off her hand.

Mission Accomplished

I [Mr. Charles Kuralt] don't have many souvenirs from my adventures on the road, but from the story of Mr. Black, I have two. The first is one of his bricks, solid and strong, like the man who made it. The second is a photograph of President Richard Nixon, standing awkwardly erect in the Oval Office flanked by Mr. Black and his granddaughter and some of the other family members. The head of the Agency of International Development is in the picture, too

As for Harvey J Witherell, the brave bureaucrat who had made this moment possible, he was in the room that day, only to find himself shoved rudely aside by a wire service photographer who said, "Excuse me, buddy, let me get through here." He stepped in front of Harvey, and so did all the other photographers. Flashbulbs were popping. Immortality in the government archives was being bestowed. In the moment of his greatest achievement Harvey had been pushed into the shadows.

But bureaucrats are nothing if not nimble. For in a corner of this photograph one other white face appears at the extreme left, wearing the insouciant expression of a man who had just elbowed his way back in the picture. It was the face of Harvey J. Witherell.

Mr. George Henry Black accompanied by his Niece Evelyn Smith went to Guyana to fulfill his mission to teach brickmaking to the villagers.

Endnotes

1. National Geographic News – African-American Food History, 2/26/2015
2. Karen Pinchin, National Geographic, Published March 1, 2014
3. Joseph E. Holloway, African Contributions to American Culture
4. Joseph A. Opala, The Gullah: Rice, Slaves, and the Sierra Leone-American Connection
5. Ibid.
6. Definition: Sluices – Webster's New World Dictionary and Thesaurus, Second Edition, Wiley Publishing Inc., 2002
7. http://www.yale.edu/gullah/02.htm
8. Joseph A. Holloway, ¶¶ 9 – 17
9. Ibid.
10. Ibid.
11. US Slave: The American Banjo and American Music, http://usslave.blogspot.com/2011/06/bonjo-african-american-music.html

Chapter Six
How It All Began: The Trans-Atlantic Slave Trade

Before its discovery by white Europeans, Africa was called the "dark continent." Although little was known about the continent, its pre-discovery developments, achievements, and innovations greatly influenced how we live today. Long before the European take over, Africa's trade in gold, minerals, and salt enabled them to accumulate great wealth and to establish orderly, cultural societies that were governed by rules.

This all changed when Europeans learned of this untapped paradise. Historian Thomas Pakenham in *Scramble of Africa* offers this confirmation. Pakenham writes that:

> "The Scramble for Africa was one of the most extraordinary phenomena in history. In 1880 most of the continent was still ruled by its inhabitants and was barely explored."[1]

However, when the treasures of Africa were exposed to the European world, five countries (Britain, France, Germany, Belgium, and Italy), inspired by greed, targeted Africa with a colonization plan that would divide and place the continent firmly in their hands.

Pakenham further tells us that by 1902 those European countries-
> "had grabbed almost all of [Africa's] ten million square miles, awarding themselves thirty new colonies and protectorates and 110 million bewildered new subjects."[2]

The Europeans, not satisfied with the conquests they were instituting, yearned for new ways to exploit this new commodity. This desire led to the Trans-Atlantic Slave Trade, a plan which resulted in the enslavement of our ancestors and deportation to New World America.

The Atlantic Slave Trade: Human History's Most Horrific and Oppressive Plan

Our ancestors who lived in Sierra Leone and Ghana prior to this brutal takeover had been warriors, accomplished leaders, skilled craftsmen and women as well as persons of note and prominence. Their history which evolved from the beginning of time spoke of the rise and fall of great civilizations.

To be captured by slave traders, humiliated, and placed in shackles was a tremendous insult, especially to our forefathers who had been known to proudly protect their families. Their women and children were now at the mercy of and subject to the sexual folly of the slave holders and the ships' crews. It was against this back-drop that this horrific enslavement plan evolved.

Triangular Trade

The Atlantic Slave Trade, also referred to as Triangular Trade, brought together economies of three continents. This was a partnership of European slave traders, African chieftains, and New World slave holders. In the 18th century, the forced deportation of millions of Africans who were torn from their homes greatly influenced the world economy.

Historical reports tell us that when early Europeans competed with one another, slavery was a prominent and accepted institution. The slave trade also ranked high over other commercial activities on the West African coast. There has been much discussion about the role of African chiefs and why they would accept the role to actively participate in a venture so destructive to their own people? The following excerpt from *History Slave Trade/ Early European Contact and the Slave Trade* gives us a glimpse and an understanding of this question:

> "To be sure, slavery and slave trading were already firmly entrenched in many African societies before their contact with Europe. In most situations, men and women captured in local warfare became slaves. In general, however, slaves in African communities were often treated as junior members of the society with specific rights and many were ultimately absorbed into their masters' families as full members."[3]

The Triangular Trade plan had a more calculated and sinister objective. Its goals were different from our forefathers' practice of slavery. The Africans granted freedom once a set sentence was completed. Instead, the horrific penalty to be inflicted upon our ancestors by their New World captors offered a lifetime sentence of servitude, torture, and free labor. Freedom came only when the enslaved person died.

The Middle Passage

AFRICANA, THE CONCISE DESK REFERENCE, gives an informative snap-shot of the African and African-American experience. Excerpts from the reference will give a vivid picture of our ancestor's horrifying treatment and the challenges they faced in order to exist and to survive the Middle Passage.

Our kinsmen, women, and children were forced to walk miles through forests, bush, and inclement weather to reach the crowded holding places near the loading docks. Before boarding the ships, they could never have imagined that their final destination could be more damnable. Our reference tells us:

> "The Middle Passage was a physical and psychological nightmare for an estimated 12 million slaves who were packed like animals aboard slave vessels. The middle or second leg of the transatlantic slave trade marked the beginning of a terrifying experience."[4]

AFRICANA and other references have talked about Olaudah Equiano, a former slave who became an activist. In his autobiography Olaudah gave his initial reaction to his capture and related his experience on the slave ship. He said, "When I looked around the ship…and saw…a multitude of black people of every description chained together, every one of their countenances expressing dejection and sorrow, I no longer doubted my fate; and quite overpowered with horror and anguish, I feel motionless on the deck and fainted."

The following excerpts give us a picture of what Olaudah and the other enslaved Africans endured during the Middle Passage:

> "Typically, Equiano and others were shackled in pairs, the right arm and leg of one chained to the left leg and arm of the other. Men were separated from the women, but all were confined below deck and packed into "slave quarters" throughout the ship's belly. These quarters were no more than six feet long and not high enough to allow an individual to sit upright."[5]

> "Conditions were miserable. Slaves were forced to lie naked on wooden planks, and many developed bruises and open sores. The unbearable heat below deck, mixed with the human waste and vomit, produced an overpowering stench."[6]

> "The unsanitary conditions were breeding grounds for diseases like dysentery, small-pox, and measles. Close to 5 percent of the slaves aboard these vessels died from disease and many more died from malnutrition."[7]

> "Slaves were fed twice a day rations of fish, beans or yams that were prepared in large copper vats below deck. Those who refused to eat, hoping to starve themselves to death, were force fed."[8]

> "Slaves were sometimes allowed, in small groups, to come on deck for exercise. Women and children were often permitted to roam freely, a practice that opened opportunities to the ship's crew for abuse and rape."[9]

> "There are more than 250 documented cases of rebellion at sea, including the Amistad Mutiny…a revolt that was the subject of a film by Steven Spielberg in the fall of 1997."[10]

A Woman of Our Time Discovers Her Link to the Middle Passage

One day, I invited my friend Fanta Coulibaly to see the VHS presentation of our family's search to find our Liberian cousins. (This is detailed in Chapter Two.) I also told her about our finding them in a most surprising place. After an extensive search and with the help of Eugenia Stevenson, a former Ambassador to Liberia, I found them living about 8 blocks from where my husband and I lived.

The presentation appeared to have triggered an experience that had been hidden deep in Fanta's memory. Fanta shared that some time ago, she watched a documentary reenactment about the Middle Passage on television. As she began to recall the event, her eyes welled with tears, and she struggled with her words. She described the scene on the boat with the men lying chained together, naked, in their own and others' body fluids. She said that the scene was so realistic and vivid that she could almost smell the stench of the bodies as the ship tossed them about on the harsh seas.

Tears began to stream down her face as she told me about something else that she remembered while watching the reenactment… Feeling her pain as we sat together, I also cried with her. Fanta continued her story by recounting how she thought she heard singing. She moved closer to the television set to investigate, and confirmed that there were women singing in the bottom of the boat. It was then that Fanta received the biggest shock. The women were singing in her Mandinka language. She also recognized what they were singing. It was a lullaby that her mother used to sing to her when she was a small child.

Fanta Coulibaly

Fanta concluded that the women were trying to help their countrymen remember their childhood days and home, despite the terrible conditions they were experiencing

These were her people who had been captured and torn from their homes in Mali West Africa by the slave traders and now were destined for the New World.

The previous discussion demonstrates that the Atlantic Slave Trade and the Middle Passage were indeed the most horrific and offensive acts against humankind in history. The only other historical event akin to our genocide is the Holocaust, which called for the extermination of the Jewish people by the Nazis. For Black people, it was an oppressive plan to dehumanize, to assure the white man's authority, and to utilize the skills and talents our ancestors brought from centuries of historical prominence and achievements in Africa.

The previous discussion demonstrates that the Atlantic Slave Trade and the Middle Passage were indeed the most horrific and offensive acts against humankind in history. The only other historical event akin to our genocide is the Holocaust, which called for the extermination of the Jewish people by the Nazis. For Black people, it was an oppressive plan to dehumanize, to assure the white man's authority, and to utilize the skills and talents our ancestors brought from centuries of historical prominence and achievements in Africa.

To establish a New World in the Americas and to maintain economies in Europe, the framers of this vicious plot, who could not accomplish these goals on their own, felt it necessary to enslave, exploit, and victimize our ancestors. What a mockery and travesty of justice.

Endnotes

1. Cover, THE SCRAMBLE FOR AFRICA-The White Man's Conquest of the Dark Continent from 1876- 1912-1st ed. Random House. Inc., New York
2. Ibid.
3. Article- History Slave Trade- Early European Contact with the Slave Trade, p.2
4. AFRICANA- The Encyclopedia of African and African-American Experience, The Concise Desk Reference, Editors: Kwame Anthony Appiah, Princeton University, Henry Louis Gates, Jr., Harvard University, Running Press, Publishers, p. 632
5. Ibid, (Paragraphs 5-10)

Chapter Seven
Arrival in Hell

I cannot imagine how our ancestors felt as they left the horrific experiences of the slave ships and rode in wagons to the plantations. Did they dare to think that life would be better than the horrendous experience of the middle passage, where they had laid shackled on boat decks, often in their own and others' body fluids, unable to move as turbulent waters raged beneath them? Women, young girls, and boys, were victimized at will and served as sexual folly for their captives. Our male ancestors, some former leaders and warriors, witnessing these atrocities, lay shackled and humiliated, unable to protect their women and children. Soon our ancestor's would find the answer to their fears and fragile hopes. The initial reception and treatment by their captives at their new plantations or farms quickly confirmed that our ancestors had truly arrived in hell.

A great-granddaughter shares the life and story of Patsy Moore who was born enslaved

Rosalie's commentary will vividly portray the horrifying and degrading lives of our enslaved countrymen and women who were of African descent.

First, I would like to share a few things about Rosalie, our narrator, who has an important story of her own. She was initially welcomed into our family as the bride of our cousin, Rev. Willie Lewis Jones. As this chapter is being written, Rosalie will be 97 years old on November 11, 2016. It is documented that her great-grandmother, Patsy Moore, lived to be between 104 and 106 years of age, according to calculations in old slave records.

Rosalie's husband, who I called "Rev.," was the grandson of Aunt Jane (see Chapter Two). She was one of the three earliest persons known to start our Bryant ancestral tree. Willie, called "Boy Jones" by the church community of Greenville, North Carolina and surrounding counties, became a minister when he was 17 years old. His extensive and inspirational ministerial career earned him an Honorary Doctor of Divinity degree from Shaw University. At his death, in 1984, he was General Bishop of The General Conference of the United American Free Will Baptist Church.

We know the saying, "Behind every great man is a woman," Rosalie was certainly "the wind behind her husband's sails," as she supported all of his endeavors. However, she also made tremendous contributions of her own. Rosalie was an elementary school teacher in Greenville, NC for 38 years. After retirement, because of her expertise and reputation, she was asked to be a substitute teacher for two more years. Her local church also valued her abilities and she served as Secretary/Treasurer as well as President of the Home Mission of her church. The District leaders, also recognized her proficiencies, and appointed her their District Secretary/Treasurer of Home Mission and subsequently President of the Home Mission Department, Free Will Baptist Annual Conference "B" Division.

It is also noteworthy to see the contributions made by our relatives and others so soon after slavery and emancipation. Becoming free, our kinfolks rolled up their sleeves to fill community and church needs and established markers for others to follow.

Patsy Moore's Life and Enslavement as Recounted by Rosalie Jones

As cousin Rosalie began to think about her great-grandmother, she remembers an alert and loving woman who was short and petite in stature. Rosalie loved being around Grandmother Patsy, as she called her, helping with chores or hearing her talk about the God she had served through the years. Realizing what Grandmother Patsy had been through as a former slave, Rosalie felt a burst of pride for the courage that her grandmother had exhibited. Rosalie couldn't imagine how anyone who was on the plantation or farm with Patsy could have tolerated and survived the horrific treatment they received from their slaveholders.

Every once in a while, Grandmother Patsy would slip up and say something about her enslavement. However, when Rosalie looked at her attentively, hoping to hear more, Grandmother Patsy always quickly changed the subject. She never really wanted to think about or to share those horrible times.

As Rosalie's great-grandmother Patsy reached her hundredth birthday, family, neighbors, and the community celebrated this milestone. It was then that the family was contacted by a local college asking permission for a few students to visit Mrs. Moore and to hear her life's story. They especially wanted to hear about her experiences when she was enslaved. Rosalie was really surprised when her grandmother agreed to visit with them. Grandmother Patsy said "I can't turn these children down if I can help then with their school work." Cousin Rosalie was especially pleased because she also would have an opportunity to hear that much guarded information.

Grandmother Patsy shared that she was born into slavery in Georgia. She did not focus on her earlier years but instead talked about a very confused and critical teenage time. The plantation was struck with a great boll weevil infestation that ravaged the cotton crops. The "grapevine" (the whisperings of the slaves among themselves), indicated that Master was about to sell off some of his slaves. He was losing so much financially and no relief was in sight from the wormy parasites.

This was a perilous time that they all knew too well. A time to wonder who would be sold off this time? Who would be separated from the kin they knew? Would they be sold into a more horrific situation, than their current daily struggle to survive? There was a saying, "It is better to stay with the devil you know than the devil you don't."

The day of anticipation and fear came and Patsy found she would be sold at the slave market. Several hearty and skilled slaves were praised by Master as prizes to be bought and Patsy and on old man, who could care for animals, were added to sweeten the deal. Patsy would be a gift for the new Mistress and would care for their baby and small children.

Patsy was sold to a plantation holder in Edgecombe County, North Carolina. It was there that she would remain until she could garner enough courage to run-a-way, north, on the Underground Railroad. This was just prior to the Emancipation Proclamation by President Lincoln.

When Patsy arrived at the plantation, the reality of this current unknown sparked new and more dominate fears. She and the others were examined to determine their value and the roles they would now assume. The enslaved who were hardy and well-built were assigned to work in the fields. Those with specialized skills in caring for livestock, machinery or household help were assigned to those areas on the farm.

Finally, Patsy was assigned to care for her new Master and his Mistress' newborn baby and other small children. Patsy grew more uneasy when she met her Mistress. Patsy immediately knew, by her Mistress' cold eyes and stern manner that she would be punished severely if Mistress was not pleased. Patsy was assigned to sleep or rest on the floor under Mistress' bed. Patsy was told to quickly crawl from under the bed if the baby or other children needed help or comfort. Patsy would pay a price if Mistress was awakened or deprived of her rest "for no good reason." During the day the children and the baby were Patsy's full responsibility.

Patsy and the other enslaved "kin" would all be up at sunrise and worked until sundown. Usually new slaves who were brought to farms or plantations immediately bonded and called each other "kinfolk" or kin. At times it was difficult to determine who was a natural or acquired relative.

In the morning they ate fatback and biscuits before going to their assigned jobs. Again at dinner time, they had fatback and biscuits. They looked forward to Christmas and the Fourth of July when they were given better meals. At times the enslaved were permitted to have small gardens to supplement their diets. Any effort to provide better clothing for themselves or to care for gardens had to be on their own time, which was extremely limited.

Heap See, but Few Know

I remember my mother often saying "heap see, but few know" and I found that this traditional saying came from her mother, Rhoda Bryant George, who had been enslaved. This saying could also have come from ancestors like Patsy Moore. They both had in their memory banks visions of terrible acts that had been inflicted upon them and their enslaved kin. As on-lookers, they were powerless to help or to intervene. It was even dangerous if they showed any indication of support or distain. When our ancestors found themselves to be the target of the abuse, their on-lookers were also unable to offer help or defense.

Patsy Moore, as she talked with the college students, indicated that she was still pained and grieved by the extreme brutality inflicted upon enslaved women. Women had no control over their lives in any way. Their bodies, children, and their men were all Master's property to do with them whatever he desired.

It appeared that Grandmother Patsy was feeling deeply moved and pained as she began to tell the students about the severe treatment woman received as they delivered their babies. Women prayed that their babies would be born at night when they were in slave quarters rather than during the day. At night they could be helped by family and kin, but during the day they were at the mercy of the "man with the whip" who supervised the birth. Grandmother Patsy explained that women who were about to give birth had to work in the fields until the baby was ready to be born. The mother was then laid on the ground, near the work area, while others watched.

An enslaved midwife and the women to receive the baby were summoned. The baby was delivered out in the open unless it was extremely bad weather. Once the baby was born and taken away by the women who would now clean the baby up and care for it, the mother was told to return to work. If some of the folks watching had concern about the mother, the man with the whip moved closer to back up his order that everyone return to work.

There were times when a mother lost a large amount of blood during delivery and could not get up on her own. Permission then was granted to others to assist her back to the work area. Unfortunately, there were times when women, suffering blood loss and other complications, died. If so the man with the whip ordered a few men to move her to the side of the road, dig a ditch, and the body was placed inside and covered over.

Any onlookers were told to return to work. No one was allowed to show any signs of grief or sadness or the man with the whip cautioned that any reaction would be dealt with by him and his whip. It was not until the workers in the field and the others on the farm were in their slave quarters that they could grieve together as family and kin.

It was also noteworthy that the new born baby was given special care. A new life born on Master's farm meant that he could see his property value rise as this baby would now owe a life time of service to him. Also he did not have to make any financial payment for this baby. It was his acquisition from the mother, whether she lived or died.

Patsy Moore also shared her concern about the practice that enslaved men and women could be contracted out to work for another slaveholder. If the Slave Master fell on hard times, he could make money by contracting one or more of his enslaved men or women out for hire. The contracts stated that the new slaveholder, after a specified time, had to give the property back in good shape or he or she could be sued. The suit was not to protect the enslaved person, but was to guarantee Master's property value. In those cases, the financial settlement only benefited the Master.

Women hired out, were often forced to be in unprotected brutal situations with no avenue of relief until the contract expired or if they were successful in escaping and returning to their permanent Master. If they returned unable to perform at their former level, Master was not usually pleased and saw them as damaged goods. As enslaved property, women were always on the losing end.

A Divisive Slave Practice: Elevation of White Skin over Black, Continues Today

Grandmother Patsy expressed how deeply pained she felt over a practice that further separated the enslaved community from one another. Namely, the elevation of light skinned slaves over dark skinned slaves which led to deeper feelings of rejection, servitude, and inferiority among dark skinned slaves. Often, when slave holders fathered enslaved girls who were born with white skin and Caucasian features, they were given special recognition or acceptance, which elicited from them loyalty and allegiance.

This created in the slave community a hierarchy and distrust between family members and siblings who had different shades of skin tones. Records described the enslaved as black (called darkies), light skinned or mulatto (which meant medium brown skin or a person who has one black and white parent).

Grandmother Patsy then shared with her listeners a story about two sisters. It is not clear whether the sisters were twins or just close in age. They both grew up in their Black mother's care in the slave quarters. They were inseparable and very devoted to one another. Both were Master's off-spring but one was dark skinned, with negroid features while the other had Caucasian skin coloring and features, much like Master and his family.

However, when the girls reached school age for the white children in the farm community, Master moved his Caucasian looking daughter into his house on the farm and she was permitted to attend school. Her dark skinned sister was denied this opportunity.

The Two Sisters Had a Secret

Both girls were very unhappy about being separated, although the white skinned sister was very pleased with her new school experience. After a while, it was evident that the two sisters had a secret. Grandmother Patsy said that everyone in the slave quarters knew the secret but this time the saying was "heap see and nobody knows." The two sisters maintained their close relationship and the sister who lived in Master's house visited regularly to see her sister and mother.

Time passed and it was time for Master to make plans for his daughter to attend college along with the white college-bound students in the community. This would also be a college where many mulatto young people attended. It was the practice of slave holders and government officials to place young girls there whom they had fathered and recognized as theirs and who, of course, looked Caucasian.

The college-bound sister felt that this was now the appropriate time for the secret to be shared with Master. This revelation possibly could keep the two sisters together. She confided to Master that for years she had been teaching her sister the lessons she has learned in school. Her sister, who was also very smart, was ready to pass the examinations. Would he please test her and give them both the opportunity to attend college together?

Master told her definitely "not" and further stated that her sister could not attend because she was dark skinned. Not backing down, she persisted, asking her father again and again. She pleaded, "Just see if my sister can pass the tests." Finally, he agreed and was surprised to find that the dark skinned sister was indeed smart and had passed the tests with very high marks.

Now the favored sister moved to the next stage in her strategy. Realizing that her father, a well-known and wealthy slaveholder, could make this opportunity available to her sister if he desired, she kept pleading. Finally, he agreed and the sisters were so pleased. They both would be attending college, but more importantly, both sisters would now receive further education.

The Sisters Received Mixed Messages in College

Once in college, the two sisters very excitedly settled in and readied themselves for classes and school activities. It was then that the dark skinned sister got a rude awakening. She was called to the office and told that while she could attend her classes, due to school rules, she could not attend any activities unless they were class related.

Both sisters were extremely hurt by this order. The sister, who was not penalized, pledged to the other that she would miss the other activities in solidarity with her. For a while, she kept her promise, but later became bored and began to accept invitations offered by classmates. This left her sister alone to fend for herself.

The dark skinned sister, however, realized that without her sister's support, she would never have been able to attend college. She decided to use this educational opportunity as a launching pad to a life in the north after graduation. She knew this was an opportunity that so many dark skinned family members and kin would never be given.

After graduation, Master's daughter returned to the farm and to Master's home for a while and then she went north to make a life for herself. Her dark skinned sister did not return, but sent word back to her mother and kin about her success at college and let them know that she would now seek a life in the North. They later heard that she was able to have a successful life and career. However, after some time, nothing more was heard from her. It became apparent that the separation initiated during college, because of a difference in skin color, had a lasting affect and put the sisters on separate paths and lives, which were never reconciled.

Slave Worship Meetings, the Launching Pad in the Quest for Freedom

Grandmother Patsy shared that the enslaved community was on the alert when something was about to happen that involved them. When they were summoned to meet in the bush for a Worship meeting, they knew that a well put together plan was about to take place.

The slave community also knew that they were not fooling Master, because he had spies who kept him up to date about their activities. Often it was one of his mulatto children who served as informant, in order to keep in the Master's good favor and to prove their allegiance. The Master's whip man was then brought in to deal a severe blow to the planned insurrection. Unfortunately, there were times when the person targeted was found dead in the bush or hanging from a tree.

Often, Master just laughed at the planned Worship meeting and said, "let them go in the bush to sing and dance, at least they are not causing some mischief." However, oftentimes it was Master who misjudged us, because everything was in place for some enslaved person or perhaps even more than one to run away on the Underground Railroad.

When this was the reason for the meeting, the person to lead the way had already arrived. At times, that person was the daughter and a former slave of the slaveholder, sympathetic to the cause of her Black people, who now put herself in harm's way to help them. This light skinned guide with Caucasian features was able to move around the farm with little notice.

The Underground Railroad conductor had been well trained for her role. As they sang, preached, prayed, and danced, she was busy instructing the ones planning to leave how to survive the treacherous ordeal. Initially, it was necessary to jump into the nearest creek; once wet it was difficult for Master's dogs to follow their scent. Grandmother Patsy was given the opportunity to run away several times but each time she was too afraid. Finally, she did gather enough courage to make the trip and was carried away to safety.

Soon after the Emancipation Proclamation by President Lincoln which freed all enslaved Black people, (Grandmother) Patsy Moore, feeling homesick for her family and kin, returned home.

Author's Note

As in Grandmother Patsy's time, the Black Church has continued to be that tower of strength and empowerment for Black people. Their quest for freedom and equal rights under the law was guaranteed by the 13th Amendment to the Constitution of the United States of America which was passed by Congress on January 31, 1865 and ratified on December 6, 1865. Although we do not know the actual dates for Grandmother Patsy's birth and death, we can surmise how she would have reacted to the 13th Amendment to the Constitution by President Lincoln. We can imagine her shouting and singing joyously "hal-le-lu-jah, see whut de Lord done!"

Chapter Eight
A Sankofa Moment in History

There are times when we look back in history to the horrifying and dehumanizing enslavement of our ancestors and we experience an overpowering desire to avenge those acts. We wish to retaliate against their oppressors. Because there is no release for our hurt and disgust we opt to "put our heads in the sands" and attempt to forget that terrible time ever happened. We can be heard to say, "why do we need to keep talking about slavery, let's just forget about that time and move on?"

However, our Ghanaian African tradition challenges us to see those horrific times as an important part of our journey. An article from *the Carter G. Woodson Center* tells us that "the word Sankofa is derived from the Akan tribe of Ghana."[1]. We also recognize that we have a tie to the Akan tribal groups through our own George family's Fanti tribe. This article entitled, *The* Power *of Sankofa* gives us the following literal translation of the word and symbol, (shown below). Sankofa means: "It is not taboo to fetch what is at risk of being left behing."[2]

This symbol drawn by our family artist, Albert Debnam, shows us a mythical bird whose feet are firmly planted forward with its head turned backwards

"Sankofa symbolizes the Akan people's quest for knowledge among the Akan with the implication that the quest is based on critical examination, and intelligent and patient investigation...Thus, the Akan believe the past serves as a guide for planning the future. To the Akan, it is this wisdom in learning from the past which ensures a strong future. The Akan believe that there must be movement and new learning as time passes. As this forward march proceeds, the knowledge of the past must never be forgotten."[3]

Our First Black President, Barack Obama, has a Sankofa Moment

What a proud moment for us as Black people to have a Black President in our lifetime. Our chapters thus far have described our history which stemmed from the earliest civilizations of humankind. We have been a proud people who has given to our world some of the earliest skills, accomplishments, and culture. Our organizational way of life, with its rules and laws, has shaped who we are today.

We lived for centuries untouched, in an era called the "Dark Ages" until the Europeans discovered us. They saw in our lives, treasurers and a way of life they could never have imagined. Instead of joining with us in a life style of sharing and relationship, their goal evolved to be one of domination and conquest. Greed continued to feed a hungry lust for power and a horrific plan was instituted to enslave this commodity, our ancestors, into human slaves. The goal, to rape our fore parents of their human dignity and to use their more advanced technology, and skills for a life time of free labor. This conceived plan would guarantee the vitality of European and New World economies for years to come.

Barack Obama

Barack Obama's biography describes him as a U.S President, Lawyer, and U.S Senator. It also gives the following facts:

> "Born on August 4, 1961, in Honolulu, Hawaii, Barak Obama is the 44th and current president of the United States. He was a community organizer, civil-rights lawyer and teacher before pursuing a political career. He was elected to the Illinois State Senate in 1996 and to the U.S. Senate in 2004."[1.] He was elected to the presidency in 2008 and is the first African American to serve in this role. He was reelected in 2012."[4.]
>
> -Text of Obama's 150th Anniversary of the 13th Amendment

President Obama presents a comprehensive and chronicled description of the last 150 years which vividly describes the slavery era, our nation's struggle with the right and wrong of it, and the moral fight against it. He challenges us not to betray the efforts of our warriors of justice – Tubman, Douglass, Lincoln and King by failing to push back against bigotry in all forms. He desires each one us to be responsible for making our lives today and tomorrow one of equality and hope, not just for our children but everyone else's children, too.

In the following, I will give headings to help define and chronical the excerpts of Obama's Text which will be included.

Obama's Opening Remarks to Congress

"The President: "In giving freedom to the slave, we assure freedom to the free." That's what President Lincoln once wrote. "Honorable alike in what we give, and what we preserve. We shall nobly save, or meanly lose, the last best hope of earth."

"Mr. Speaker, leaders and members of both parties, distinguished quests: We gather here to commemorate a century and a half of freedom- not simply for former slaves, but for all of us."

"Today, the issue of chattel slavery seems so simple, so obvious – it is wrong in every sense. Stealing men, women, and children from their homelands. Tearing husband from wife, parent from child; stripped and sold to the highest bidder; shackled in chains and bloodied with the whip. It's antithetical not only to our conception of human rights and dignity, but to our conception of ourselves – a people founded on the premise that all are created equal."[5.]

To many of that time the judgement against slavery was also clear

"Preachers, black and white, railed against this moral outrage from the pulpit. Former slaves rattled the conscience of Americans in books, in pamphlets, and speeches. Men and women organized anti- slavery conventions and fundraising drives. Farmers and shopkeepers opened their barns, their homes, their cellars as waystations on an Underground Railroad, where African Americans often risked their own freedom to ensure the freedom of others. And enslaved Americans, with no rights of their own, they ran north and kept the flame of freedom burning, passing it from one generation to the next, with their faith, and their dignity, and their song."[6.]

Reformers passion made the protectors of the status quo to dig in more

"For decades, America wrestled with the issue of slavery in a way that we have with no other, before or since. It shaped our politics, and it nearly tore us asunder. Tensions ran so high, so personal, that at one point, a lawmaker was beaten unconscious on the Senate floor. Eventually war broke out- brother against brother, North against South."[7.]

"At its heart, the question of slavery was never simply about civil rights. It was about the meaning of America, the kind of country we wanted to be- whether this nation might fulfill the call of its birth: "We hold these truths to be self- evident, that all men are created equal, that they are endowed by their creator with certain unalienable rights, "that among those are life and liberty and the pursuit of happiness."[8.]

President Lincoln's challenge to make good on the birthright promise

"President Lincoln understood that if we were ever to fully realize that founding promise, it meant not just signing an Emancipation Proclamation, not just winning a war. It meant making the most powerful collective statement we can in our democracy: etching our values into our Constitution. He called it "a King's cure for all the evils."[9]

After hundred and fifty years, were our ancestors really free?

"Progress proved halting, too often deterred. Newly freed slaves may have been liberated by the letter of the law, but their daily lives told another tale. They couldn't vote. They couldn't fill most occupations. They couldn't protect themselves or their families from indignity or from violence. And so abolitionists and freedmen and women and radical Republicans kept cajoling and kept rabble-rousing, and within a few years of the wars end at Appomattox, [10.] we passed two more amendments guaranteeing voting rights, birthright citizenship, equal protection under the law."[10.]

"And still, it wasn't enough. For another century, we saw segregation and Jim Crow make a mockery of these amendments. And we saw justice turn a blind eye to mobs with nooses slung over trees. We saw bullets and bombs terrorize generations."[11.]

Through dangers, toils, and scares and yet the call for freedom survived

"We hold these truths to be self-evident." "And eventually, a new generation rose up to march and organize, and to stand up and to sit in with the moral force of nonviolence and the sweet sound of those same freedom songs that slaves had sung so long ago — crying out not for special treatment, but for equal rights. Calling out for basic justice promised to them almost a century before."[12.]

"Like their abolitionist predecessors, they were plain, humble, ordinary people, armed with little but faith: Faith in the Almighty. Faith in each other. And faith in America. Hope in the face so often of all evidence to the contrary, that something better lay around the bend."[13.]

"Because of them — maids and porters and students and farmers and priests and housewives — because of them, a Civil Rights law was passed, and the Voting Rights law was signed. And doors of opportunity swung open, not just for the black porter, but also for the white chambermaid, and the immigrant dishwasher, so that their daughters and their sons might finally imagine a life for themselves beyond washing somebody else's laundry or shining somebody else's shoes. Freedom for you and for me. Freedom for all of us."[14.]

At last, its Commemoration and Celebration Time

"And that's what we celebrate today. The long arc of progress. Progress that is never assured, never guaranteed, but always possible, always there to be earned — no matter how stuck we might seem sometimes. No matter how divided or despairing we may appear. No matter what ugliness may bubble up. Progress, so long as we're willing to push for it; so long as we're willing to reach for each other."[15]

Obama's challenge for today: Do not let fear and cynicism hinder progress

"But we betray our most noble past as well if we were to deny the possibility of movement, the possibility of progress; if we were to let cynicism consume us and fear overwhelm us. If we lost hope. For however slow, however incomplete, however harshly, loudly, rudely challenged at each point along our journey, in America, we can create the change that we seek. (Applause.) All it requires is that our generation be willing to do what those who came before us have done: To rise above the cynicism and rise above the fear, to hold fast to our values, to see ourselves in each other, to cherish dignity and opportunity not just for our own children but for somebody else's child. (Applause.) To remember that our freedom is bound up with the freedom of others — regardless of what they look like or where they come from or what their last name is or what faith they practice. (Applause.) To be honorable alike in what we give, and what we preserve. To nobly save, or meanly lose, the last best hope of Earth. To nobly save, or meanly lose, the last best hope of Earth. That is our choice. Today, we affirm hope.

Thank you. God bless you. May God bless the United States of America. (Applause.)"[16]

A Sankofa Moment of recognition for Abolitionist Harriet Tubman: Our abolitionist, the new face of the $20 bill

We now see recognition given to one of our own, Harriet Tubman, who, through the years, has been cited in history books, Black history classes and programs. Her many acts of heroism confirmed that she had rescued over 300, men women and children from their horrific lives in slavery and brought them north to freedom on her Underground Railroad. The term Underground Railroad described a network of abolitionists, who were called railroad agents. These agents offered their lives to help enslaved black people escape from farms or plantations in southern states.

The New York Herald, in1907, described a typical escape led by Harriet Tubman:

> "On some darkly propitious night there would be breathed about the Negro quarters of a plantation word that she had come to lead them forth. At midnight, she would stand in the depths of woodland or timber swamp, and stealthily, one by one, her fugitives would creep to the rendezvous. She entrusted her plans to but few of the party…She knew her path well by this time, and they followed her unerring guidance without question. She assumed the authority and enforced the discipline of a military despot."[17.]

Our reference tells us that Tubman used many tactics to keep her groups moving to freedom:

> "She drugged crying babies with paregoric, an opium derivative, boarded southbound trains to confuse slave hunters; assumed various disguises; leading the weary and frightened fugitives in singing spirituals; and threatened to kill escapee who tried to go back by pulling out her revolver and shouting at them, "move or die!" …Tubman made her last Railroad trip in 1860, after South Carolina seceded from the Union and before civil war broke out in the United States."[18.]

The, article, *Harriet Tubman Ousts Andrew Jackson in Change for a $20- New York Times*, gives us a detailed and vivid understanding of how historic and dramatic this decision was for us as Black people and our nation. Some excerpts from the article by Jackie Calmes reads as follows:

"Washington- Treasury Jacob J. Lew on Wednesday announced the most sweeping and historically symbolic makeover of American currency in a century, proposing to replace the slave holding Andrew Jackson on the $20 bill with Harriet Tubman, the former slave and abolitionist, and to add women and civil rights leaders to the $5 and $10 notes."[19.]

"But the broader remaking of the nation's paper currency, which President Obama welcomed on Wednesday, may well have captured a historic moment for a multicultural, multiethnic and multiracial nation moving contentiously through the early years of a new century."[20.]

"Tubman, an African-American and a Union spy during the Civil war, would bump Jackson- a white man known as much for the common man- to the back of the back of the $20, in some reduced image along with the White House. Tubman would be the first woman so honored on paper currency since Martha Washington's portrait briefly graced the $1 silver certificate in the late 19th century."[21]

Our Bryant /George family, looking forward in a new era, with feet firmly planted on the ground, can truly celebrate a Sankofa moment as we look back to our ancestor's enslavement in this country. Our family and others, have survived the most horrific enslavement of a people in human existence. Yet, we can see as we resurrect our history, just how much our ancestors persevered against the racial, torturous, and bigoted tides against them.

However, we can now embrace the pride, recognition, and celebration that has come in our life- time. Our nation, could elect a Black president Barack Obama to its highest office. The United States could also honor a Black woman, Harriet Tubman, by placing her face on its $20 bill. This former slave and abolitionist has finally been validated for her courage, tenacity and devotion as she sacrificed her life to free her people as the Chief agent of the Underground Railroad, and as she served as a Union spy during the Civil War.

Endnotes

1-3   Article, *The Power of Sankofa-Carter G. Woodson Center*, Berea College, Berea Kentucky. Ibid. ¶. 1-3
4-16   FW: *Text of Obama's 150 Anniversary of 13th Amendment- Message*
17-21   New York Herald-1907

Chapter Nine
Two Worlds - The Captives and the Enslaved

Introduction

This chapter will acquaint us with our Bryant ancestors and the Quinerly family who enslaved them on a farm in Henrahan, North Carolina. It will briefly detail historical facts about slavery in North Carolina. We will also gain a vivid understanding of what our Bryant family encountered when they landed in North Carolina, from the slave ships, far away from their native country, Sierra Leone.

An article, *The Growth of Slavery in North Carolina*,[1] offers some important insights. It tells us slavery became a part of North Carolina's history in the late 1600s and early 1700s when Europeans settled there. The first slaves were brought from the West Indies but a greater number were brought from Africa. It was further indicated that record-keeping was non-existent, which created an identity vacuum for our ancestors. Some direct quotes from the article are as follow:

> "Records were not kept of the tribes and homelands of African slaves...so it's impossible to know the exact ethnic make-up of North Carolina's slave population."

North Carolina's geography (which includes several small islands) hindered its role in the early slave trade. The article further states:

> "The string of Islands that make up its Outer Banks made it dangerous for slave ships to dock on most of North Carolina's coast and most slave traders chose to dock in ports to the north or south of the colony."

The one exception to this inability to dock slave ships was Wilmington on the Cape Fear River. Due to this port's accessibility and the increased demand for slave laborers, Blacks outnumbered whites 2 to 1 by the 1800s.

> "The town relied on slave's abilities in carpentry, masonry, and construction as well as their skill in sailing and boating, for its growth and success."

> "By 1767, there were about 40,000 slaves in the colony. About 90 percent of these slaves were field workers who

performed agricultural jobs. The remaining 10 percent were mainly domestic workers, and a small number worked as artisans in skilled trades, such as butchering, carpentry, and tanning."

It is important to note that despite the fact that records were not kept to identify enslaved persons, very careful and detailed records and laws were enacted to control enslaved blacks. The following are some of these laws:

"The North Carolina Slave Code of 1715 required slaves to carry a ticket [eventually known as a "pass"] from their master whenever they left the plantation. The ticket stated where they were traveling and the reason for their travel. The 1715 code also prevented slaves from gathering in groups for any reason, including religious worship, and required whites to help capture runaway slaves."

"A second set of even stricter laws was put in place in 1741. These laws prevented slaves from raising their own livestock and from carrying guns without their master' permission, even for hunting. The law also limited manumission or freeing of slaves. It stated that a master could only free a slave for "meritorious services," and even then the decision had to be approved by the county court."

"Perhaps the most ominous of all the laws was the one regarding runaway slaves. It stated that if runaways refused to surrender immediately, they could be killed and there would be no legal consequences."

"Slaves, themselves could be brought to trial in a slave court, which was separate from the regular court system. This court had the authority to try, sentence, and even execute slaves without trial by jury. The accused slaves had no representation, and could not call witnesses to defend themselves. During the colonial period, about 96 percent of slaves tried in these courts in North Carolina were convicted."

"In addition to these public courts, each plantation or farm had its own private system of justice in which individual slaveholders dealt out punishments they felt were appropriate. Slaves were usually only brought to slave courts for what were considered the most serious crimes, such as murder, theft from a white person or assault on a white person."

Our Earliest Known Bryant Family members

Our Bryant family history began with three siblings, Noah, Jane, and Rhoda. Slave calculations confirm that the siblings were born in the 1850s. Their slaveholders operated a farm located in Henrahan, NC, not far from the towns of Ayden and Grifton, in Pitt County, North Carolina.

There appear to be no other known family members so we surmise that other members born on the farm were sold. An article, *The Life of a Slave*[2], confirms this probability:

> "The slave trade in North Carolina separated countless husbands, wives, and children. On a whole, slaveholders cared little about the kindred bonds of slaves and tore families apart by selling slaves for profit."

> "Because the larger plantations of the lower south needed more slaves than the smaller farms of North Carolina, it was not uncommon for slaves in the state to be sold to slave traders who took them south to Georgia, South Carolina, Mississippi, Louisiana or Alabama. Once a family member was sold and taken to the Deep South, they became almost impossible to locate or contact."

It is important to note that although we had some information about our Bryant family members, the only information we had about the George family was that Edward Dudley George, husband of Rhoda George, came from Jones County, North Carolina.

Lucinda Fox Ward, who initially began the search for our ancestors, desired to see where this project could lead and gave us the name Bryant/George Family. The birth certificate of Lucinda's mother, Julia Bryant George, confirmed that Julia's father, Edward Dudley George, came from Jones County, North Carolina.

In 1976, Lucinda called all the relatives she could find to the New York Sheraton Hotel. At this first Family Reunion, Lucinda challenged us to join with her to determine "Who we are as a family?"

In the fall of 1984, Lucinda learned that she had terminal cancer. Concerned about the project that meant so much to her, Lucinda asked that I continue the pursuit to determine our family history and linage. After years of searching and exploration, this book of our findings has been completed.

This has truly been a loyal and devoted family effort. I extend heartfelt thanks and appreciation to the many family members who have participated in this project, which has bonded us into a loving and wonderful family. We also give honor to God who has been our Covenant partner in this effort.

Lucinda included the following quote from Plutarch, the Greek historian, biographer, and essayist in our first reunion program: "It is indeed a desirable thing to be well descended, but the glory belongs to our ancestors."

The Quinerly Family, our Bryant Slaveholders

We have learned from family records and personal knowledge that the linage of the Quinerly family in North Carolina began with Patrick Quinerly (d. Aug. 26 1833) who came from Ireland with his brother. He married Martha (d. April 3, 1840) and they had one son.

Forgotten Places Pitt County- Part II[3] by Roger Kammerer tells us that "there was a village called Quinerly, named for W.A. Quinerly, who owned a store there with someone named Brooks, as early as 1877. A post office was established on February 9, 1894. It was also reported that 1897 was hard on the merchants of Quinerly and on February 27, 1897, the store of J.W. Quinerly and Brother burned. It was felt that the fire was caused by an arsonist in retaliation against W.B. Quinerly who had killed a man in Greenville the week before. Sometime thereafter, the J.W. Quinerly and Brother store was moved to Ayden, North Carolina."

The Quinerly Family's Letters about an Enslaved Man Named Sam

Slave narratives provide a unique voice to people from whom, historically, we rarely hear. This author is greatly honored to be able to present three narratives which show the interaction between the Quinerly family and an enslaved person on their farm. This author was over joyed to find that the J.Y Joyner Library at East Carolina University in Greenville, N.C. had been recipients of the Quinerly family letters.

During research at the J.Y Joyner Library, I was assisted by staffer Bobby Green. We painstakingly examined and read each letter in two containers of correspondence. Many letters and records were related to historical events and financial transactions. We felt as if we were searching for a needle in a haystack. However, we did not come away empty-handed. We found three letters which showed a Quinerly slave owner's interaction with an enslaved man whose name was Sam.

The Letters

The following letter gives us a glimpse into the family's activities in Annie Quinerly's, the apparent slaveholders, absence. She is hospitalized in Richmond Virginia. This letter was sent to Annie's by her daughter Argent, who shares that her father is working hard with the potato harvesting and Sam, the enslaved Negro, has stepped up to take care of the family chores and responsibilities. In the conversation, there does appear to be a concern that Sam be satisfied.

Above, the writer's name is not clearly written. A census report which I have been fortunate to find (shown below) identifies the writer as Argent Quinerly, a female, born in NC, who was probably a teenager when this first letter was written.

1860 Census Report

Name:	Argent Quinerly
Residence:	Pitt, North Carolina
Age:	26 years
Estimated birth year:	1834
Gender:	Female

Second Letter

In this second letter, Argent is writing on behalf of a younger cousin, Millard, who joined the household about a year ago. It is Millard who reports on Sam's duties and activities. Mischievous little Millard further comforts his grandmother by sharing that he has not played any tricks on old Sam. From this letter we get an understanding of the life and happenings of the slaveholder's farm.

POPLAR BRANCH CHAPTER
YOUNG TAR HEEL FARMERS
POPLAR BRANCH, N. C.

May 29, '30

Dearest "Am-Ma":

Last year, in honor of this day, you wrote to me, so this year I am a big boy and am going to write to you. You know Daddy and Mother tell me I have been here just a year but it seems to me I have been in my home longer than that. If I always learn as much each year as I have this year I believe I will be the smartest grand-child you have. Well I can nearly walk and I talk all the time, the folks just don't understand. I am like you Am-Ma, I like to hear the birds sing about five o'clock in the morning. All these grown-ups here don't like for me to get up so soon but I call them out just the same.

WILLIAM DUNTON, President	MANLY LEE, Secretary	MERRILL EVANS, Advisor
COPELAND NEWBERN, Vice-Pres.	LINDSEY HAMPTON, Treasurer	EMORY SMITH, Teacher

Poplar Branch Chapter
YOUNG TAR HEEL FARMERS
Poplar Branch, N. C.

Mother has made a bed room out of it, and I sleep in the back room, so I do not bother him until about eight or eight thirty.

Uncle Sam has been mowing the lawn, working the garden and helping Mother out doors. He built a shelf in the kitchen and painted a table today. I believe he likes to stay here right good but don't think he likes me much. He is so afraid I will do ugly tricks when he has me. Aunt Margaret gives us a lot of milk so we are making him drink his part. He went swimming yesterday and decided he would wait until the water got warmer before going again.

Daddy is working hard now with potatoes. I don't see him if left early in the mornings.

[Note- omitted sentence- "Momma is well so she, Sam and I are playing …"]

playing and having a good time.

Ann-Ma one hopes you hurry and get well. He wants you to come see me and stay long old time.

He kiss you right now,
Your big little boy, Millard.

P.S. Mamma don't worry over Sam. We are getting on fine. He seems very well satisfied.

Love
Argent.

Third Letter

Our final letter gives a conversation between Annie Quinerly and her friend John who advises her regrading financial matters. Annie has fallen on hard times and could lose the farm, if she does not make the right decisions. John suggest that Annie hire Sam out, a common practice in those times. She would be financially compensated for Sam's services and this could help or save the farm. The author wishes to note in some of those "hiring out agreements," the enslaved worker was forced to endure horrific treatment, long hours of labor, and was never recognized or compensated for the sacrifice they were making.

Our Matriarch, Aunt Jane, and the North Carolina Bryant Family

Aunt Jane, and siblings, Noah and Rhoda, were enslaved on the Quinerly farm. Every family member has played an important role in our history, so when a new relative or kin has joined us, it has been celebration time. At each reunion, one of our nine branches have assumed leadership for the reunion format, activities, and has presented their history. The highlight of our Family Reunion, July 20- 22, 2012 was the presentation of the Two Volume Journal spearheaded by JoAnne Stanback. It was entitled *Yesterday Today*

Tomorrow and was given to all in attendance. This contribution enabled family members to see themselves on our family tree, notable highlights of their lives and contributions. Material from JoAnne's journals will be cited as we discuss the family ties beginning with Aunt Jane. JoAnne is the great niece of Aunt Jane and is the author's daughter. In subsequent chapters we will also share more about Noah and Rhoda.

We will begin this discussion of our North Carolina family with Jane Bryant who was one of our earliest Bryant ancestors. She was the matriarch that kept the family together. She was the guiding force who shaped and molded the family and kin into a survivable unit. One that was able to surpass the horrific challenges that confronted them. It was also Jane who placed her faith in the "God of the Israelites" who would now be with her family, in this life and the next.

Jane Bryant Jones (born 1851): After her siblings migrated north, Jane remained in North Carolina and kept our southern tradition alive. She was the foundation of our North Carolina family and her life symbolized perseverance, wisdom and love. Jane was Grandma and Aunt to many and she was that open door for all relatives and kin to enter.

After the slave shacks had been taken away and new houses built with several rooms, the Bryant homestead offered us a family meeting place with Jane firmly in charge. She was that loving nurturing spirit that kept up with everyone. As was cited in (Chapter Two), when it was time for a new baby to arrive, the mother moved in with Aunt Jane so that she could be offered Jane's assistance, support, and perhaps Jane also delivered the new born.

All who knew Aunt Jane loved and respected her. She was that motivating force that gave the generations that followed: purpose, direction, and the desire to make a difference in the lives and communities where they lived.

Jane had two sons Columbus (Man) Jones and William Augustus Jones, Columbus Man Jones married and they had a daughter Ava Mae Jones

Ava Mae Jones: When the family moved to Ayden, Ava Mae lived close to her cousins, the children of Will Jones. She was remembered as a lively, warm and devoted family member. She would assemble all the family members who were called kin, for large Fish Fries at her home. One summer, Lucinda and I brought Cousins Betty and Elizabeth George from New York to visit their southern family. Ava Mae coordinated a large family reception to greet and meet us upon our arrival. This loving gathering was filled with down home goodies, as we hugged and shared information about our family tree. What a wonderful Fish Fry that was, one which I always remember with fondness.

Will Augustus Jones married Elizabeth Quinerly and they had five children shown in the picture below.

Annie Jones, Cleo Jones, Rhoda Jones Darden and Willie Lewis Jones. Steven Jones is not shown. Note: the Quinerly enslaver probably was Elizabeth's father because she was given the Quinerly last name.

Aunt Janes Grandchildren, were the Bedrock and Foundation of our North Carolina Family

Growing up, when Lucinda and I visited N.C., these were the cousins that I looked forward to seeing. I was their little cousin, Rhoda Jane, named for my grandmother Rhoda, and our family matriarch Jane. Because I was the youngest of the group, I deeply felt their protective love and care.

Annie (b. July 13, 1924) and I were inseparable whenever we visited one another. She and Rhoda Darden were devoted sisters. Although Annie had a lovely home across the street from Sister Rhoda's home, she stayed with Rhoda most of the time. Rhoda's was the home place where all the action occurred. Annie assisted her older sister whenever there was a need. She had a green thumb and cultivated a lovely garden in the back of Rhoda's house ready to compliment any meal being served. When Rhoda's health began to fail, it was Annie who cared for her.

Steven was always close to me and we had a special relationship. He said that he remembered when I was born. When he was inducted into the Army for World War Two, we were in constant contact. He also enlisted me to write to friends he met who did not families or close ties. I was so happy when he traveled to Washington, DC, after he was discharged from Service. Steven later decided to leave the farm to make a life for himself, up North.

Cleo was that conservative, warm, reliable cousin, who you could look up to for guidance. Cleo was forever dapper and distinguished, actually I cannot recall a day when he was not dressed in a suit and tie. He and his wife, Mandy, lived nearby to Cousin Rhoda Jane and were always on hand for all family events. Unfortunately, they never had children of their own but lovingly raised and educated a neighborhood young boy, who needed a family.

Lewis, was my mentor and teacher. I remember the day when he took me to view the various routes, our family members took when they bravely ran-away from the farm. I personally revisited the water-ways they crossed to get away from the approaching dogs. He pointed to the deep cuts in the trees left by family members to show where they once existed.

I looked forward to Rev's revivals. His unique technique of preaching usually depicted the life of their rural farm community. He talked about the strutting hen, who ruled the farm-yard or the devious fox, to highlight the roles some of the members in the audience might also be playing. As, we walked along the roads, the next week, people were still laughing because they saw themselves in what he had said.

Before going to a revival, Rev, always gave me a lecture. He instructed me to just take a little bit of food at each home that we visited. He was expected "Pop-call", after the revival and to bring his visiting relatives along. When I visited, there was nothing else like the good southern foods and the deserts, wow. I ate and ate and always that night when I got home was "sick as a dog" as the old saying goes. I never learned Rev's lesson and paid dearly, too.

Traditionally Black folks, and maybe other folks too, pass family names from one generation to the next. There were so many relatives named "Rhoda" in my generation, unfortunately, only Rhoda Darden and I survived. Rhoda Jane Darden became the successor and the North Carolina Family Matriarch when

Aunt Jane passed away in 1926, a year after my birth. Her home then became that place to go to for comfort, a chat, or to have a cup of tea with a newly baked piece of cake/pie.

I was always eager to arrive early for a gathering so that I could not only have samplings of food ahead of time, but watch Rhoda preparing our special dishes. One time in particular I watched her prepare her delicious homemade rolls. With the greased pan in front of her, she selected a spoon full of dough and placed it within her fist, she gave a gentle squeeze, and the dough, went through the air and landed in its proper place in the pan. She could actually, look toward me while talking and continue the process, until the pan was lined up, full of the newly prepared rolls. This old southern technique, passed down from Aunt Jane, seemed like magic.

Rhoda was a devout Christian and worked in various roles in the church. Many in her community of Ayden sought her words of wisdom and advice.

Willie Jones, the young minister, gave the Commencement Address at his sister, Annie's High School Graduation (Annie is fourth, starting from right)

Aunt Jane's Dreams Sets the Stage for a Grandson's Achievements

Our Family's Special Salute to Bishop Willie Lewis Jones

Pioneer, Minister, Community Leader

Willie Lewis Jones, Bishop of the United American Free Will Baptist Church, was born in Grifton, N.C., April 5, 1916. He received his earlier education from Pitt County Schools and graduated from the South Ayden High School.

At age 15, Willie was called to the ministry and was ordained October, 1932. In 1942 and 43, Willie was selected "Pastor of the Year" by his church's Northeast "B" Division and he also received the Conference Scholarship to Shaw University, Raleigh N.C. He attended Shaw University (1941-45), and subsequently, studied at the Kingsley Correspondence School of Religion, Astoria, Oregon. In 1960, Willie received a Bachelor of Divinity (BD) degree, and in 1972, received an Honorary Doctor of Divinity (DD) degree, both from Shaw University, Raleigh, N.C.

Answering God's call, Reverend Jones served churches in the following North Carolina counties: Pitt, Greene, Lenoir, Nash, Beaufort, Craven, and Martin. In his role as Bishop, the following offices were held: President of the District Union Meetings for 18 years; President of the Young People's Christian League Convention for 12 years; Vice Bishop for 5 years; Bishop of the Northeast Annual Conference 'B" Division for 23 years. All of the above mentioned offices were on the Annual Conference level. He also held offices on the General Conference level. He was Chairman of the Adjustment Committee (now known as the Executive Committee) for 3 years; Financial Secretary for 5 years, and Bishop for 20 years.

Our cousin, Willie Lewis Jones wanted to help his parishioners and neighbors, to have better housing, so he led the St. John Free Will Baptist church in building a housing development, named St. John Village. There were 19 buildings, with residence facilities for 96 families, on 10 acres of land. At that time in history, it was unheard of for a black church in a rural community, like theirs, to able fund a building program, costing approximately two million, one hundred and fifty dollars.

Bishop Jones still had another giant dream to be realized. He wanted to leave as his legacy the construction of a United American Free Will Baptist denominational Tabernacle and Headquarters, in Kinston, N.C. God truly blessed him, and before his death in 1984, his dream Tabernacle, with a seating Capacity for 1,500 parishioners was realized. It also served the denomination well as its headquarters.

These passages were often read as affirmation to us by Dr. Jones: "We rejoice in the great truth that we have been called into the church of God, by our Heavenly father. We bear witness to the truth that God is in Christ reconciling the world unto Himself. Our witness consists not only in what we say, but also in what we do."

Reflections of Our American Family- Our Roots and Heritage

Reverend Rhoda C. Nixon, Family Coordinator

When I think of three words that symbolize us as a family and are the hallmark of who we are, the words are survival, service, and celebration.

Many family members and I were born on a little farm in Henrahan, near Ayden, North Carolina. Whenever I visited the farm to see it and to take pictures, the residents (whether black or white) welcomed me. Southern tradition and culture places great emphasis on one's birthplace and roots.

From my earliest recollections, our family has been a close-knit and dedicated community. On my Grandmother Rhoda's side, it was the Bryants and on my Grandfather Edward Dudley's side, it was the Georges.

My cousin, Lucinda and I always looked forward to visiting North Carolina to enjoy the delicious meals, to attend revivals at our cousin, Reverend Louis Jones's church, and to gather information about our family's history and tradition.

I can recall when the word-of-mouth Southern community was as efficient as our telephone and e-mail are today. Arriving in Greenville, Lucinda and I would immediately go to the farmhouse where our sweet potato pies were cooling on the table waiting for us. After eating our pie, we would go to the Quinerly farm, where our family lived and worked. We would find them planting and harvesting cotton, tobacco, soy beans and corn. It was wonderful to celebrate our being together by enjoying cool, sweet watermelon straight from the vine.

Our cousins Annie and Rosalie shared that in the 1960's life changed drastically for economic reasons. North Carolina, once leading in the production, use and exportation of tobacco in the Unites States, suffered stiff regulations by the government. It was determined that many of the poisons and chemicals used for plant diseases and insect pest control were injurious to human health.

Our family like many others were sharecroppers who planted crops on land rented l from a landlord. Mr. Quinerly, our Landlord was also our family's former slaveholder. Due to his financial losses, because of government regulations, Mr. Quinerly, raised the price to be paid by our relatives, for tools, food, and fertilizer. Although Mr. Quinerly was to share 50/50 the money received from crop sales, our relatives share grew less and less. Mexican laborers were also brought in because they provided cheaper services. With improved mechanical technology to harvest cotton and tobacco, sharecropping as a means of work and survival was now in jeopardy.

Our relatives began to take whatever jobs were possible in nearby Ayden. Other relatives moved north to seek work and survival. As new plants and industries came to the South, our family in Ayden and surrounding townships began to work at DuPont (a maker of nylon), Burra's Welcome (a producer of medicines), TRW (an automobile parts manufacturer), and a local cucumber factory.

Becoming more financially stable, our relatives bought homes and settled into a lifestyle of city living. When I visited my family, I enjoyed seeing their progress and the contributions they were making to their new communities.

Endnotes

1. The growth of slavery in North Carolina- North Carolina Digital History, Provided by UNC Libraries, pp. 1,2
1. http://www.learnnc.org/lp/p/editions/nchist-newnation/5252
2. The life of a slave- North Carolina Digital History, Provided by UNC Libraries.
3. http:/www.learnnc.org/p/editions/nchist-antebellum/5602
4. Forgotten Places Pitt County, Part 11 by Roger Kammerer (Willie Lewis Jones- 788)

CHAPTER 10

The History and Legacy OF NOAH BRYANT AND HIS FAMILY

Through numerous pictures, announcements, letters, and biographical sketches, this chapter tells the story of the history and legacy of Noah Bryant and his family. Each personal profile and item of memorabilia has its unique way of contributing to the legacy.

The Bryant Generations and Legacy

Andrew & Ellen Bryant

Our Bryant family line originates with Noah and his sisters, Jane Bryant Jones and Rhoda Bryant George. They lived in Ayden, North Carolina and are our earliest recollections of our ancestors after emancipation. Noah was a legend in Pitt and Craven Counties. He was called "the teacher" and was known for his fight against illiteracy. He was one of the few Blacks who could read and write and he traveled throughout the counties teaching others.

Census accounts verify that the Bryants lived in the middle 1800s. Matriarchs in their own rights, Jane and Rhoda, Noah's sisters, were the foundations of the families they formed.

Andrew, Noah's only child, and his wife Ellen, had three children: Roberta, Andrew, and Roland. They lived in Washington, D.C. Andrew, Sr., considered a "Jack of all trades" was also a well-known electrician. Ellen was a seamstress.

Roland, Roberta and Andrew Bryant

The Bryant children grew up and were educated in Washington D.C. Roberta and Roland graduated from Dunbar High School; Andrew Jr. graduated from Armstrong High School and Howard University. Each made their mark professionally: Roberta in the federal government; Roland, like his father, became an electrician; Andrew Jr. became an architect.

Roland Bryant Sr. had five children–Roberta, Nadine, Linda, Ronda, and Roland Jr. Andrew Jr. had one son, Andrew III. Together they comprised the second generation of Bryants.

The third generation of Bryants from Roland Bryant Sr. is composed of twelve children: Stacey and Rodney Downs; Steven, Colleen, and Carla Martin; Jamie and Kimberly Lett; Brandon, Kiama, Roland III, Micheco and Francesco Bryant.

A fourth generation of Bryants has begun with the birth of Magdalene, daughter of Steven Bryant and Adora Martin.

THE BRYANT – GEORGE 2006

FAMILY REUNION

Welcome to Our Celebration!

Hostesses: Ronda Bryant and Roberta Bryant Faulks

Special Salute

On behalf of my sister, Roberta and me, we welcome you, our family and friends to the 2006 Family Reunion. It is hard to believe that two years have passed since our last reunion when we gathered in Germantown, Maryland. Out last family reunion was hosted by our Liberian cousins. We are honored to be your hostesses for this year's reunion. Welcome one and all!

It will be exciting and interesting to catch up on everyone's endeavors and adventures during the past years. Since we last met, I have been fervently working to obtain my Bachelor's degree in nursing by May 2007. I don't plan to stop there! My career goal is to receive my Master's degree as a nurse anesthetist. Yes, I have my work cut out for me! Roberta and her husband Walter work for the state of Michigan. Roberta is an officer at the women's prison and Walter is a counselor for the Michigan mental health services.

As the reunion nears, our only regret is that our father, Roland Bryant, Sr. is no longer with us to join in the festivities. He passed prematurely from congestive heart failure on August 14, 2004 at the age of 73. Many times following the reunion of 2004, he recounted special memories of the 2004 Family Reunion that he held dear to his heart. It was his first reunion and, regrettably, his last.

Our father often asked when were we going to start planning for our next reunion, which he eagerly wanted to attend. Our father had one wish: that his daughters (Roberta, Nadine, and Linda) could know their family's history and legacy. He can now rest in peace because his eldest two daughters and former wife will be travelling with us. We welcome them with open arms and hearts. Our father may not be with us in the physical world, but I am certain his spirit will travel with us as we venture to the Bahamas.

The Bryant family will truly be represented in full force this year. We welcome my brother, Roland, Jr., his long-time love Veronica, her daughter April, and Roland III. Roland III is a high school senior. Roland, Jr. is an avid photographer and has been designated "official Cruise Videographer." My son, Frank, is attending Wayne State University and is working toward a degree in Electrical Engineering. He is following in the footsteps of his Grandfather Roland and Great-grandfather Andrew.

I am delighted and honored that my mother, Violet, is joining us. She has been anticipating getting to know one and all.

In closing, we gather in our father's memory knowing that he is smiling down upon us as we sail to the Bahamas in love, laughter, and peace.

        Love,

        Ronda L. Bryant

Roland Basil Bryant, Sr.

Our Cruise Captain"

At the Bryant-George 2004 Family Reunion Celebration, Roland Bryant, Sr. quickly volunteered to host our 2006 Family Reunion Celebration. He had a wonderful time enjoying the activities provided by our Liberian cousins. He danced and danced, met new relatives and friends, and Roland brought his children (Ronda and Roland, Jr.) and grandchildren (Frank, Kiama and Roland, III) to the 2004 Celebration. . He so wanted to bring more Bryants into the fold. His wish has now come true because many more of his family and extended family, the Jenkins, are with us for this Bryant-George 2006 Family Reunion Celebration.

Roland Basil Bryant was born in Washington, DC on July 23, 1931. He was the youngest of three children born to Andrew and Ellen Bryant. His siblings, Roberta and Andrew, predeceased him. Growing up, Roland experienced a loving family, until he lost both parents as a pre-teenager.

The family, devout Christians, attended New Bethel Baptist Church where Roland's great aunt, Rhoda Bryant George, and other relatives were charter members.

Roland was a gifted and innovative youngster. As a young man, Roland left Washington to seek work in Harlem, New York. There he met and married Cynthia Harleston. Of this union, three daughters were born: Roberta, Nadine and Linda. Later the family moved to Detroit, Michigan. Eventually this marriage ended in divorce.

Roland served in the Armed Forces and was stationed in Honolulu, Hawaii as an aircraft mechanic. It was in Hawaii that he met and subsequently married Violet Kakuno. Of this union two children were born Ronda and Roland, Jr.

Following in his father's footsteps, Roland founded the Bryant Electric Company. He and Violet were partners. Violet managed the administrative details. Roland was responsible for supervising projects.

The company became successful and secured projects from city, county, state and federal agencies. Roland became the first black electrical contractor in Detroit to be responsible for street lighting.

Roland became well-known and respected in Metropolitan Detroit for his professional skills. Concerned that minorities were not offered opportunities in the City of Detroit, he organized and became president of the Minorities Contractors Association. He and other contractors became a support system for each other.

As we view the legacy that Roland has left for us, we are proud that he was one of us. His good humor, dedication and love for us challenge us to build the best lives that we can. We, therefore, pay tribute to Roland Basil Bryant, Sr. and salute him as our 2006 Cruise Captain.

The Tie That Binds
Leonard and Roberta Jenkins

Leonard Jenkins and Roberta Bryant were married almost 50 years before God took Roberta home. Leonard now resides in a nursing facility in Maryland, but is doing well. Leonard and Roberta were very dedicated to both their families—the Jenkins and the Bryants. They ushered a close bond that has united and made these two families one. We salute Leonard and Roberta for all that they have been to us. We welcome all our Jenkins family who are with us for this celebration.

Obituary of Roberta Bryant Jenkins

Roberta Ann Bryant Jenkins was born January 7, 1923 in Washington, D.C. from the union of Ellen Jones Bryant and Andrew D. Bryant. She always demonstrated great love and affection for her family and friends and instilled in others her enthusiasm when working on an array of committees and programs.

Roberta attended J.F. Cook Elementary School, the Old Terrell Junior High School and Dunbar High School, where she graduated from in 1940. Always a diligent worker and a bright student, at a young age she participated in many school activities. For this reason she was chosen to present a token of appreciation to the great Civil Rights Leader, Mary McLeod Bethune, after her appearance at Terrell. While a student at Dunbar, the family lost their mother. Her brothers, Andrew and Roland, will always remember the love and understanding she displayed in holding the family together.

It was during this time that she met her future husband Leonard, also a student at Dunbar. After graduation, she left Washington, D.C. to work for the War Department in Newark, New Jersey and returned to Washington, D.C. to enter into a beautiful marriage that was to last for almost fifty (50) years. When he enrolled in Cornell University, they moved to New York, where she later took an active role as a member of Brooks Memorial Methodist Church. Displaying great zest and vitality, her participation as a worship leader, in Christian education, and her work with children in tutorial sessions and crafts endeared her to other members of the church.

When they retired, Roberta and Leonard returned to Washington, D.C. after a 30 year absence. Immediately she sought a small intimate church and found Sharp Street United Methodist where feeling a keen need for involvement, joined the choir and outreach programs.

As a talented seamstress, she enjoyed making outfits for her relatives and friends and was proudest of a dress that she made for the Sister of Sinbad the Comedian and another one worn by a friend to a recent affair at the White House.

Having just returned as a Lay Delegate to the annual conference of The United Methodist Churches, she had just completed and turned in her report when she was called by a family friend for help when God called her home.

Roberta Ann Bryant Jenkins beloved wife of Leonard R. Jenkins; sister of Andrew D. Bryant of Washington, D.C. and Roland B. Bryant of Detroit, Michigan. She is also survived by many nieces and nephews; an adopted sister, Rev. Rhoda Carrison Nixon of Adelphi, Maryland; five sisters-in-law, Elsie W. Bryant, Arnita and Teresa Jenkins of Washington, Violet Bryant of Detroit, Michigan and Mildred Jenkins Harris of Temple Hills, Maryland; two brothers-in-law, Eldelbert and Wainwright Jenkins of Washington, D.C. and many relatives and friends.

She was a dedicated member of the following clubs; Kappa Silhouettes, Dunbar High School Class of 1940, Brookland-Woodridge Chapter No. 2414 of the AARP and the Rolling Spring Home Owners Association. Surely your days of goodness on this Earth will be dearly remembered and will always comfort us whenever we grow sad thinking of you!

Obituary of Andrew Daniel Bryant

Andrew Daniel Bryant was born in Washington, District of Columbia on December 27, 1929 to Andrew and Ellen Bryant. He was the second of three children. Andrew died on Sunday, November 3, 2002 at the Washington Hospital Center, following a life filled with personal success, professional accomplishments, and civic contributions.

Andrew's early life with his close-knit family was changed tragically when both of his parents died before he was 9 years old. Although he was left without the special love and guidance of a mother and father, he was academically talented and strongly motivated to make the very best of his circumstances. Andrew excelled in school, and, early on, developed a love of architecture. His scholastic ability and interest in design led him to enroll at Howard University, where he was awarded a full scholarship to the School of Engineering and Architecture. He earned a Bachelor of Arts degree in Architecture in 1953.

Following graduation, Andrew served with distinction as a First Lieutenant in the United States Air Force. He was honorably discharged at Griffiss Air Force Base in Rome, New York, after a two-year tour of duty that included assignments in Guam and Okinawa.

Andrew returned to Washington after his military service to begin the requisite three-year apprenticeship and training for his professional license. Upon completion of this requirement, he formed the architectural practice of Byrd and Bryant with the late David R. Byrd. In 1966, he established his own general architectural practice, where he remained active until the sudden onset of his illness in August 2002.

Andrew's practice drew clients from government entities, the military, the private sector, and non-profits. Commissions from the District of Columbia Government included the design of schools, libraries, homes for the elderly, bridges, and public housing. The U.S. Navy sought his assistance for projects in Riverside, California and Houston, Texas. He also performed work for the Washington Metropolitan Transit Authority; for private developers of shopping centers, housing and commercial centers; for churches, nursing homes, a masonic fraternity's national headquarters, and for his alma mater.

As a Life Member of Kappa Alpha Psi, which he had pledged during his undergraduate years, Andrew was greatly honored when his beloved fraternity selected him to design Kappa Alpha Psi's National Headquarters in Philadelphia. He was also honored to serve, on occasion, as a visiting architecture design critic at Howard University and at The University of the District of Columbia.

In addition to his professional accomplishments, Andrew had a distinguished record of civic contributions. Locally, he served as president of the District of Columbia Architectural Registration Board; president of the District of Columbia Chamber of Commerce for two years; and member of the District of Columbia Building Industry council. Andrew was appointed to the District of Columbia Citizen's Zoning Advisory Board in 1969 by Mayor Walter Washington and later, by Mayor Marion Barry, to the District of Columbia's Residential, Commercial and Institutional Structure Fire Protection Study Commission. He also served, by appointment, on the Rivlin Committee, the District of Columbia Stadium Board, and two re-election task forces.

Andrew was especially proud of two aspects of his early involvement in civic lifer. One was the opportunity to serve as Chairman of a tournament conceived to bring together local golfers and celebrities to play golf as a means of raising money for the United Negro College Fund. Although this fundraising format is widely used now, it was an innovative and untested approach at the time. Fortunately, with assistance from two major sponsors- National Cash Register and Coors- the tournament attracted over 330 golfers and raised what was then the substantial sum of more than $60,000.

The other especially satisfying experience was Andres's work with the Anthony Bowen YMCA, where he served for twelve years as a member of the Board of Directors. He later served on committees established to organize the construction of the Metropolitan YMCA built at 17th Street and Rhode Island Avenue, NW.

On the national level, Andrew was a past Director of both the American Institute of Architects and the National Organization of Minority Architects. He was also a member and early activist fighting for professional rights for minorities in the National Technical Association. Later on, President William Jefferson Clinton invited Andrew to the White House to discuss his proposals for the National Alliance Fair Trade Agreement.

Andrew always felt unusually privileged to hold membership in various social clubs, including The What Good Are We; The Hellians; The Guardsmen; and the National Negro Golf Association. He also was a member of Sigma Pi Phi Fraternity; Epsilon Boule. His membership at Indian Spring Country Club allowed him to pursue golf, which was one of his favorite pastimes.

Andrew's marriage to Carol Cheltenham, the mother of his son, Andrew, ended in divorce. A stepson, Ernest Simmons, died in 1989. He is survived by Elsie, his devoted wife of 41 years.

Through the years, it has been wonderful to see our "branches" grow as marriages have brought new kin into our fold. We now celebrate the Jenkins family who has been with us from our inception. We are also proud to share Wain's greetings to announce his family's plan to host the next family reunion.
The Jenkins Connection
Greetings

From Master and Mistresses of Ceremony Wain Jenkins, Vivian Jenkins and Dana Jenkins

It is with greatest pleasure that we, the Jenkins Connection, host the 2008 Bryant-George Family Reunion in Laurel, Maryland. Our families go way, way back. The Jenkins and The Bryant-George family connection began when our Uncle Leonard Jenkins met Roberta Bryant in high school in Washington, DC. After their marriage, our families became one and spent many memorable times together. Leonard and Roberta moved to Long Island, NY where their hospitality was extended to the Jenkins family and the Bryant family throughout the years. We all have memorable experience shared at 121-32 Benton Street- tours of the Big Apple, including the World's Fair, many Yankees games and World Series. Between New York, Washington, Detroit and everywhere in between, our lives have been a part of a big loving family that has been there for each other and through events such as our bi-annual reunion, will continue to do so for years to come.

We are also pleased to have been a part of past Bryant-George Reunions and were especially delighted when we found our George ancestors from Liberia. Finding our Liberian Connection has made us all feel great about our ancestry and ties to the continent of Africa.

The last reunion, hosted by Ronda and Roberta, will go down as an experience to remember for all time. As we all cruised to the Bahamas, a great time was had by all. This year we have some surprised and acknowledgments as we honor the Patriarchs of the family, past and present.

Let us remember that through strength, family and the love our God, all blessings flow.

Wain Jenkins

The Bryant-George 2006 Family Reunion Celebration
July 12, 2006

Dear Family,

It has been our pleasure to serve you as your Bryant-George 2006 Family Reunion Celebration Committee. It has been wonderful to sail the seas to the Bahamas and to enjoy one another. We have been committed to strengthening the bonds and ties of our family and to celebrate our rich legacy.

We acknowledge with deep appreciation all who have come from far and near to share this time together. As we near the end our Celebration and plan to return to our homes, our prayers are that God will always bless and preserve our family.

Again, we thank you and we love each of you.

Ronda L. Bryant, Co-Chairperson

Roberta Bryant Faulks, Co-Chairperson

Roland Bryant, Jr. Committee Member

Barbara Howell, Committee Member

Mary Jenkins, Committee Member

Oliver Jenkins, Committee Member

Rhoda C. Nixon, Family Coordinator

Gerald Smith, Committee Member

Mary E. Tipton, Committee

Chapter Eleven
A New Era in History

As we reflect back on our journey, we can celebrate the findings of our years of study of who we are. Our lives have been greatly influenced by those who came before us. We all reflect the past struggles, challenges, achievements, and contributions of our ancestors on whose shoulders we stand.

Every new era of history has a catalyst that confronts that time and brings about change. Daniel Paul speaks to this in his book: *First Nation History Abraham Lincoln – Slavery Abolished.*

> On September 22, 1862, United States of America President Abraham Lincoln issued the preliminary Emancipation Proclamation, declaring all slaves in rebel states should be free as of January 1, 1863. This did not mean people of color had suddenly become United States citizens that held equal rights to those held by Caucasians, Lincoln expressed his thoughts on it. He said "I think the authors of that notable instrument (Declaration of Independence) intended to include all men, but they did not intend to declare all men equal in all respects. They did not mean to say that all men were equal in color, size, intellect, moral development or social capacity."…However, this Proclamation was radical enough that it was the basis of the American Civil War. We find that slaves and former slaves played a critical role in the Union victory and in securing freedom.[1]

In *Remembering Slavery*, edited by Ira Berlin, Marc Favreau, and Steven F. Miller, we learn that the enslaved now emboldened by the Emancipation Proclamation took flight from the farms and plantations to seize this possibility for freedom and joined the Civil War. Because of their courageous and valiant efforts, the Union victory was accomplished.

> They tell us that slaves, by escaping their owners, undermined the Confederate war effort by working inside federal lines; they advanced the Union cause by serving the Union army and Navy. They assured the Federal army's battlefield triumph… Their enlistment assured their freedom and helped to liberate enslaved relatives friends, and neighbors.[2]

Just as the Emancipation Proclamation was a catalyst in our nation's history, it was a forceful influence in the history of my family. My grandfather was one of those who played a role in the evolution of our family and of our nation. It is with great pride and gratitude that I share with you the story of my grandfather and his role in our nation's struggle to ensure freedom for all.

A Mishap Turns Into a Blessing

Throughout this book, we have indicated that Edward George's history had continually eluded us. However, finally an occurrence that seemed like such an inconvenience, turned out to be a blessing in disguise. The author and her assistant were finally wrapping up visits to places of interest to find family information. Once home and reviewing the Quinerly Family letters (noted in a previous chapter), we found the Archive's copier had chopped off the bottom of the letters. Although completely drained and exhausted, we returned the next day to the University of North Carolina (UNC) to have the letters recopied.

While looking for the letters again in their containers, a tall White man came up and said, I have noticed you here and have wondered what you are doing? I shared with him my life-long pursuit to find our family's history. The man extended his hand and said my name is Roger Kammerer, can I be of service to you? I almost fell off my chair; this was the well-known historian everyone had told me about and had wanted me to meet. I said to him "everyone has wanted me to contact you and God has brought you today."

The rest is history. When I returned the day after Thanksgiving and kept my appointment with Mr. Kammerer, he had found my grandfather, Edward George, who had served in the Civil War. Since that time, the relationship between me and Roger has evolved into a treasured friendship and he graciously wrote the wonderful Apprentice piece which begins this book.

To set the stage for my grandfather's story, let us first look at the era my grandfather and others like him sought to change. With hope deep in their hearts and souls, they escaped from farms and plantations in North Carolina to join the Civil War. Believing in a God whom they felt would protect them, they dared to feel this pursuit would be a path to freedom not only for themselves, but for others who walked in their shoes.

The Legacy of Edward George Who Served in the Civil War

My grandfather was born enslaved on a plantation in Jones County North Carolina. As a young man, he broke out of bondage. It was the summer of 1863 and the Civil War was drawing to its climax. Edward George decided to fight for his freedom and the freedom of his people.

Through the years, my family and I have attempted to resurrect information about our ancestors. This was an especially difficult task because slaves had no records to identify themselves by name. Slaves were considered as property and were listed on bills of sale according to their value. They could have been listed as Negro - $4,000, Negro - $600, Negro - $1,700 or Negro - $400.

With the help of Roger E. Kammerer, a noted genealogist and historian in North Carolina, I was able to learn that my grandfather ran away from the plantation to the safety of the Federal forces in New Bern, NC. He was enlisted in the Union Army on June 2, 1863 by Captain Croft. He enlisted for three years' service as a private in Company K, 25th Regiment, United States Colored Infantry. Company K became part of the 1st Regiment US Colored Infantry.

A book, *History of Colored Troops in the American Civil War*, revealed that:

> Approximately 18,000 African Americans, comprising 163 units served the Union Army during the Civil War and many more served in the Navy. Both free African Americans and runaway slaves joined the fight. On July 17, 1862, Congress passed two acts allowing the enlistment of African Americans, but official enrollment occurred only after the September 1862 issuance of the Emancipation Proclamation. By August 1863, 14

Negro Regiments were in the field and ready for service.³

Mr. Kammerer's information and my follow-up exploration at the National Archives in Washington, D.C. revealed that when my grandfather signed up, he was a twenty-year old laborer with dark eyes, dark hair, and a dark complexion who stood 5 ft., 7½ inches tall. He was on the muster roll from June 30, 1863 to April 30, 1866.

As I look through my grandfather's muster rolls, I began to feel a real connection to him. I began to envision how he must have looked when he answered "present" to the call of his name to receive his paycheck. He kept losing equipment and had to pay for a haversack, canteen, shelter tent, and letters.

Edward George was in several engagements. He was wounded in a battle at Olustic/Olustee, Florida on Feb. 20, 1864. He was in a skirmish at 10 Mile Station, Florida on June 2, 1864 and he was in another skirmish at Darby's Station, Florida on Aug. 12, 1864. He fought in the battle of Honey Hill, South Carolina on November 30, 1864 and was in a skirmish at Deveroux's Neck, South Carolina on December 7, 1864.

He was mustered out of service on June 1, 1866 in Charleston, South Carolina. He was last paid on December 31, 1865, with $38.24 still due.

The Washington Post's article Civil War 150, dated Sunday, April 28, 2013 cites the pay disparity between black and white troops. It states,

> Before Black men joined the army, Secretary of War Edwin Stanton gave assurances that they would receive $13 per month, the same as white troops. However, after seeking legal counsel, the War department announced that Congress authorized that Black men be paid only $10 per month. Despite the verdict, Black men continued to join the Union Army in large numbers. In the last months of the war Congress resolved the disparity and issued back pay.⁴

Edward George made application for his pension on August 28, 1884 in Washington D.C., as an invalid. (Application No #521180.) His wife Rhoda George filed for his pension on January 12, 1899 in Washington, D.C. as his widow (Application No #682953). My mother, Susie, the youngest of their 16 children was about seven years old when her father died.

With pride and admiration, I pay tribute to my grandfather, Edward George, for his service to our country. Even after being wounded in his first skirmish, he fought on, enduring four more engagements before retiring as an invalid. He served with dignity and valor in this nation's struggle to ensure freedom and justice for all. I love you and salute you, Grandpa.

The History of Jones County Where My Grandfather Was Enslaved

To gain an understanding of the time when my grandfather was enslaved in Jones County, the following gives us a snapshot of its founder and a nation in its infancy.

Willie Jones, the Founder of Jones County

The *"North Carolina History Project"* – Willie Jones, 1741 – 1801 tells us about the Jones County's Founder, Willie Jones, and his deep feelings about our Nation's Constitution

> Willie Jones was an influential Jeffersonian states' righter and patriot during the Revolutionary War and Federalist periods. Willie Jones pronounced (Wiley) is remembered mostly for opposing the Ratification of the United States Constitution. His political influence has had a lasting influence.
>
> Once a new constitution was submitted to the states for ratification, Jones vigorously opposed its adoption…Jones opposed ratification, for he feared the Constitution created a standing army, a supreme court that overruled states decisions, and a federal government that regulated the economy to benefit a few commercial interests. To Jones the Constitution was a dangerous instrument of centralization; and to keep it from doing so, he wanted the document to enumerate specific, individual rights. Until such a list

was included, Jones encouraged his colleagues not to ratify the Constitution.

In great part because of Jones's influence, the state of North Carolina remained out of the Union in 1788. But returned when it ratified the Constitution in 1789 and because of Jones and men like him, the Bill of Rights was eventually adopted.

Willie Jones was the quintessential aristocratic planter. His Halifax County plantation consisted of approximately 9,900 acres and 120 slaves. He defended liberty during the American Revolution (1776-1783).[5]

The Daily Life of the Enslaved

We can imagine the life experience of the aristocrats like Willie Jones, but it is really difficult to imagine the horrific lives that my grandparents and other slaves experienced on the North Carolina plantations and farms. It was like living in two different worlds at the same time. Following are some of the experiences of those enslaved as recorded in *The Life of a Slave* provided by UNC Libraries.

> Daily life for a slave in North Carolina was incredibly difficult. Slaves, especially those in the field, worked from sunrise to sunset. Even young children and the elderly were not exempt from these long hours. Slaves were generally allowed a day off on Sunday and on infrequent holidays such as Christmas or the fourth of July. During their few hours of free time, most slaves performed their own personal work. The diet supplied by slave holders was generally poor and slaves often supplemented it by tending small plots of land or fishing. Many slave owners did not provide adequate clothing and slave mothers often worked to clothe their families at night after long hours of labor.
>
> One visitor to colonial North Carolina wrote that slaveholders rarely gave their slaves meat or fish and

that he witnessed many wearing only rags. Although there were exceptions, the prevailing attitude among slave owners was to allot their slaves the bare minimum of food and clothing; anything beyond that was up to the slaves to acquire during their very limited time away from work. Shelter provided by slave owners was also meager. Many slaves lived in small stick houses with dirt floors, not the log slave cabins often depicted in books and films. These shelters had cracks in the walls that let in cold and wind and had only thin coverings over the windows. Again, slave owners supplied only the minimum needed for survival; they were primarily concerned with keeping their financially valuable slaves alive and working rather than providing for their comfort, health or safety.[6]

As mentioned earlier, my grandfather Edward was born in Jones County and oral history tells us that my grandmother Rhoda was born in Pitt County. Maps show that Pitt County is next to Craven County and it was in 1779 that a portion of Craven County became Jones County. I have often pondered and wondered how it might have been possible that my grandparents, who lived on two different farms, could have met one another and formed a relationship. Perhaps my answer comes from *The Growth of Slavery in North Carolina after the Revolution* which tells us:

> The social dynamic of slaves in North Carolina was somewhat different from their counterparts in other states, who often worked on plantations with hundreds of other slaves. In North Carolina the hierarchy of domestic workers and field workers was not as developed as in the plantation system. There were fewer numbers of slaves to specialize in each job, so on small farms, slaves may have been required to work both in the fields and at a variety of other jobs at different times of the year. Another result of working in smaller groups was that North Carolina slaves generally had more interaction with slaves on other farms. Slaves often looked to other farms to

find a spouse, and travelled to different farms to court or visit on their limited time.[7]

It should be noted that this was a cooperative plan by the two slave owners. The bonding of the slaves and the subsequent births gave them a ready-made increased labor force. They also saved money by not having to buy more slaves. It also should be noted that the site where my grandmother was enslaved was called the Quinerly Farm. However, the destinations, plantation and farm, seem, at times, to have been used interchangeably.

My Grandmother Rhoda's Story Joins with Edward George

My grandmother, Rhoda George, for whom I am named, and her two siblings, Jane and Noah, were born on a farm in Hanrahan in Pitt County, North Carolina in the mid-1800s. Roger Kammerer, in an article in the *Greenville Times*, April 1990 tells us how Hanrahan got its name and describes its earliest community. This article can also be found in the *Forgotten Places in Pitt County Part II*.

> Harahan, a small community north of Grifton was located near Littlefield and was four miles from Centerville. Hanrahan was named for James A Hanrahan (1831 – 1891) who had a store there as early as 1879. This was a well-known agricultural area that grew a lot of rice and wheat. There were also many apple and peach orchards.[8]

My grandmother Rhoda was born in 1852, her sister Jane in 1851, and her brother Noah, the oldest, in 1842. These birth dates have been calculated using census reports and oral history.

My grandparents were born at a most important time in our nation's history, a time called the Decade of Crisis. This was also a time of nation building in which some states were found to be either joining the Union or seceding from it, based on the issue of slavery. Many states were champions for the abolishment of slavery while others wanted the lucrative business of slavery to continue. The evolution of this conflict is still reflected in our governance today and is cited in the *1850's: Decade of Crisis* (http/www.doc1850.webs.com/).

Fugitive Slave Act was passed in the Compromise of 1850. It declared that all runaway slaves be brought back to their owners/masters. Anyone caught helping these slaves out would be fined $1,000 and be subject to months in jail. There was huge opposition to this law. Northerners protested and caused riots because they feared slave power conspiracy or they just didn't want slavery. White southerners watched with anger and alarm as their supposed 'victory' in the Compromise of 1850 became basically meaningless.[9]

Uncle Tom's Cabin is a book written by abolitionist Harriet Beecher Stowe.

It is one of the most influential books ever written. It quickly became a best seller and sold thousands of copies within the first year. Stowe was revered by many in the North but was despised by many southerners. This book brought a huge message about anti-slavery and abolitionism and made an enormous affect.[10]

The *Decade of Crisis* also tells about how our political system was evolving as it attempted to relate to slavery:

> The main purpose of the Kansas-Nebraska Act was for Stephen A Douglas to create opportunities for the transcontinental railroad he wanted. Due to the argument against the northern route west of the Mississippi, he introduced a bill in January 1854 that would organize a new territory called Nebraska. This would open a white settlement in an Indian populated area. Douglas knew this would cause problems in the south because it would create a free state. In an effort to make things even, he inserted a provision that the status of slavery in that area would be determined by popular sovereignty. Because southern Democrats demanded more, Douglas agreed to repeal the Missouri Compromise and split the area into two

territories – Nebraska and Kansas. Kansas would be a slave state. (This would give each side a state of support.) This would become the Kansas-Nebraska Act and President Pierce supported the bill and it became law in May 1854 e.

The legislation had many ominous consequences. It divided and completely destroyed the Whig party that officially disappeared in 1856. It also divided the northern Democrats, many of whom were appalled at the repeal of the Missouri Compromise because they considered that a sacred part of the Union. That made a big impact because many of them left the party.

But most importantly, this new party made a new party. The Republican Party was formed of Anti-Nebraska Democrats and Anti-Nebraska Whigs in 1854. It quickly became a major force in American politics. In the elections of that year and more, they won enough seats in Congress to organize the House of Representative, with the help of their allies, the Know-Nothings.[11]

After Emancipation: The Story Continues
It was helpful to examine the two worlds, that of our Nation's leaders and the world of our enslaved African ancestors. The political leaders, on differing sides, really wrestled with having a conscience and a soul or just continuing a program that enslaved others for their many benefits. Could or should they risk giving up a commodity that was the foundation of their economy, wealth, and power?

Endnotes

1. *First Nation History Abraham Lincoln- Slavery Abolished by* Daniel Paul
2. In Remembering Slavery, edited by Ira Berlin, Marc Favreau, and Steven Miller History of Colored Troops in the American Civil War, Americancivilwar.com/histofcoloredtroops.html
3. *The Washington Post, Civil War 150*, Sunday, April 28, 2013
4. *The North Carolina History Project- Willie Jones,* 1741-1801
5. *The Life of a Slave,* provided by UNC Libraries (University of North Carolina)
6. *The Growth of Slavery in North Carolina after the Revolution* http://www.learnnc.org/lp/pages5252
7. *The Greenville Times, April 1990, Forgotten Places in Pitt County, Part II,* (Both references carry the article- How Henrahan got its Name by Roger Kammerer)
8. *1850's: Decade of Crisis* (http/www.doc1850.webs.com)
9. *Uncle Tom's Cabin,* by Abolitionist, Harriet Beecher Stowe

Chapter Twelve

Edward and Rhoda George's Story, Inspired by Census Reports

Earlier census reports give a remarkable roadmap and bits and pieces of history to help develop Edward and Rhoda George's story.

Free at last: Lincoln issues the Emancipation Proclamation, January 1862.

1870 CRAVEN COUNTY EIGHT TWSP

Schedule 1- Inhabitants in Swift- Creek Township, County of Pitt, June 1880

Name	Relationship	Age	Profession, Trade, Etc.
George, Edwair		35	Working on farm
Roada	Wife	28	Keeping house
John	Son	10	(not legible)
Julia	Daughter	7	
Aima	Daughter	5	
Tincey	Daughter	3	
Nathaniel	Son	1	

Note: Although names were often misspelled and/or were not readable, these reports help confirm facts about our earlier ancestors.

151

1900 Census, Washington, D.C. Champlain Avenue

Name	Date of Birth	Place of Birth
Rhoda George, widow, had 16 children, 8 now living	May 1850	
Julia	March 1872	NC
Nathaniel	August 8, 1877	NC
Edward	March 1881	NC
Millie J	April 1885	DC
Susie	November 1892	DC.

1910 Census, Washington, D.C. Champlain Avenue

Name	Age	Place of Birth	Status
Rhoda George	55		16 children
Annie M. Jones	34	NC	Married to Uriah Jones
Millie J. Carter		DC	Married to Edward G. Carter
Susie G. Ross	18		1 child married to Tucker D. Ross
Tucker D. Ross	21	VA	Mulatto
Mildred Gertrude Ross	8 months		Mulatto
John W.S. Chapman	45	NC	Living in home

1920 Census, Washington D.C. Champlain Avenue

Name	Age	Place of Birth	Status
Rhoda George	72	NC	
Tinsey Corbert	40, born 1880		Daughter, Kitchen Maid
Richard Corbert	45		Laborer- Hotel
Andrew Bryant	26	IL	Nephew, Auto Mechanic
Ellen Bryant	22	DC	Maid
Susie Ross	26		Divorced, Maid
Mildred Ross	10½		

After Emancipation and Freedom Edward and Rhoda George's Journey Begins.

To recap some of the background for this journey, we must look back to Edward's life prior to the above census reports. It was in 1862 that Abraham Lincoln issued his preliminary Emancipation Proclamation which declared all slaves in rebel states to be free as of January 1863. According to Edward's service records, at age 20, he ran-away from the farm where he had been enslaved and enlisted into the Union Army. The Civil War was drawing to its close. Historians say that the enslaved and former slaves played a critical role in the Union Army's victory. It was Edward's desire to ensure his freedom as well as freedom for his people.

The census reports offer us an important and interesting narrative. We see Edward and Rhoda in Craven County, North Carolina and it is the year 1870. We also know that Edward enlisted in the Army for three years, so with his pledge completed, he apparently was able to begin his life with Rhoda.

The 1870 census shows that the couple had established a homestead and had two children. Edward was listed as a farm laborer and Rhoda was keeping house. Their youngest child Nathaniel was 4 years old and the oldest Sally was 7½. We can surmise that perhaps Edward and Rhoda began a family before he enlisted in the army, because of Sally's age. There is also a question concerning Sally, because there is a letter possibly (d) by her name that is marked over. Did that mean that Sally was deceased? She is not listed again in the subsequent census reports. I have often been told that some of my grandparent's children died while quite young. Times were hard and epidemics and nonexistent medical care caused many adults and especially children to perish.

Ten years later, 1880, we find the family has moved to Pitt County in Swift-Creek Township, North Carolina. Edward is still working doing farm work and Rhoda is keeping house and caring for their children. They have five children now ranging from 10 to 1. Their names are John, Julia, Aima, Tincy, and Nathaniel.

By the 1900 Census, our family has moved to Washington, D.C. and live on Champlain Avenue in the Meridian Hill section of D.C., (often referred to as the "Hill"). We remember that Edward was injured in the war in his first skirmish and was adjudged an invalid when he was mustered out of the Army. Edward is missing in this report so we conclude that he is deceased as Rhoda is shown as head of household and is listed as having only 8 living children out of the 16 previously mentioned. Julia and Nathaniel were again mentioned and Edward, Millie, and Susie were added. If we add Tincey, John, and Aima (which also could have been mistaken for Annie) we now account for eight children.

Ten years later we find Rhoda was age 55. There was also an Annie Jones who was married to Uriah Jones. Millie was married to Edward Carter and Susie, age 18, was married to Tucker Ross. The couple had an 8 month old baby girl, whose name was Mildred. Richard Corbert and W.S. Chapman were listed as living in Rhoda George's home.

The 1920 Census has the family still living on Champlain Avenue. Rhoda was now age 72 and Tinsey and her husband were both living in the home. We now also see Andrew Bryant and his wife Ellen as residents. My mother Susie was now age 26 and divorced and my sister Mildred was 10½.

Oral history has told us that Noah Bryant, after emancipation, traveled to Illinois to seek a successful life. He fell in love with a white woman, which was taboo in those days. A son, Andrew was borne out of this relationship. As was the custom in that time Andrew was carried to NC and Rhoda was asked to raise him. Wherever Rhoda has lived, Andrew has been with her. Now we see both he and his bride living with Rhoda. My mother, Susie, and Andrew and Ellen always had a close relationship and their oldest daughter Roberta and I developed a close relationship as well. We acted more like sisters. Roberta, two years older than me, was very protective especially when I began kindergarten at the same school.

These census reports have, despite some errors, provided a roadmap to follow the actions of Edward and Rhoda after the Civil war. We see their beginnings as a young couple and can actually follow them (through census reports) as they and their family age.

Rhoda and Edward's Family Picture Gallery

These pictures give us a glimpse into the past allowing us to actually see how some of the Bryant/George children looked. We also see how baby Mildred, who was only 8 months old in the first census noted, looked when she became an adult. I was pleased to find a picture of Edward Carter, my Aunt Millie's husband, as well as two other Bryant relatives with whom my mother and our family kept in close contact as I was growing up.

Julia George Fox
(Mother of Lucinda Fox Ward and Milton Fox)

Millie George Carter

Nathaniel George

Edward George Jr.

Susie George Ross-Carrison

Mildred Gertrude Ross
(Daughter of Susie, pictured above)

Edward (Eddie) Carter

Cousin William (Bill) Bryant

Cousin Henry Bryant

Chapter 13
The George Sisters Share Their History and Legacy

JOHN GEORGE AND AMY KENNEDY GEORGE

Parents of Edward Dudley, George Nettie, George Chadwick, Johnnie George, Fannie George Fulcher, Robert George, Sallie Ann George Rhoades, Samuel George, Sennie George Riddick, Nathaniel George

The George Sisters

A granddaughter, Geraldine Rhoades, tells us about Sallie Ann George and her descendants.

Sallie Anne George (1882? -1933), daughter of Amy Kennedy and John George, was born in the state of North Carolina. At 14, she married Anthony Rhodes who was also born in North Carolina. They had two children, Daniel McKinley and Fannie, when they moved to the Tanners Creek section of Norfolk at the beginning of the 20th century. Anthony worked in the shipyards and Sally gave birth to seven more children: Jesse, Herbert, Addie, Arthur, Lillie, Anthony, Jr., and Eulah. (The youngest child may have been Elaine's mother.)

The family moved to 133rd Street in Harlem sometime around the middle of the 1920s. Anthony worked as a longshoreman. Only four children were living at home at that time, Arthur, Lillie, Anthony, Jr., and Eulah. Sallie Anne and her sister, Seenie, were members of St. Mark Holy Tabernacle when they decided to go to Bible School and prepare for the ministry. When they graduated, they were called evangelists because, at that time, women were not ordained as ministers in the United Holy Church of America, the denomination to which church belonged. In the middle of January 1933, Sallie Anne developed pneumonia and was admitted to Harlem Hospital.

Four days later, on January 19, 1933, she died and was laid to rest in Woodlawn Cemetery on January 22, 1933. One of her daughters-in-law, Mabel Allen Rhoades, would later recall that "Mother Rhodes" was the "sweetest woman that ever walked in shoe leather." The eight grandchildren of Sallie Anne and Anthony are: Daniel McKinley, Jr., Miriam Elizabeth, Elsie, Virginia Sally Ann, Mabel A., Elaine, Lillian, and Geraldine.

Sallie Anne's legacy of ministry continued with her son, Arthur (1908-1938). According to his testimony, God called Arthur while he was at Harlem's Savoy Ballroom. He left the dance floor and found his way to his mother's church where he gave his life to the Lord. He later became a minister and was one of the "Sons of Thunder," a name given to a trio of young ministers who were known throughout the Northern District of the United Holy Church of America for their dynamic preaching. Arthur could also sing and would often end his sermons with his signature song:

> How about you, how about you,
> I hope my Savior is your Savior too.
> I've said Lord, take and use me.
> That's all that I can do.
> I gave my heart to Jesus.
> How about you.

Arthur married Mabel Virginia Allen, the superintendent of St. Mark's Sunday school, in 1932 and not long after that, he changed his last name from Rhodes to Rhoades. Just as his ministry was really developing, Arthur died of pneumonia in 1938. He was survived by his widow, who was pregnant with their fourth child (Geraldine), two preschoolers (Miriam Elizabeth and Virginia Sally Ann), and one toddler (Lillian). Fifteen years after his death, people still remembered him and would tell his youngest daughter, Geraldine, that "Your father could *preach*" [their emphasis, not mine] and then continue with "If I heard that Brother Rhoades was preaching, I'd be there."

The desire to minister and serve continued in Arthur's children, who were raised in Harlem. As young people, they were active in their respective churches. Miriam was secretary of the Young People's Holiness Association for the New York District of the United Holy Church of America, Virginia eventually became the youngest president of the Christ Crusaders at the Soul Saving Station, Lillian was superintendent of the Sunday school at the same church and, for a time, worked at the church's mission in Haiti. Geraldine, a member of New Covenant Temple, was primarily interested in child evangelism and was a member of the teaching staff of the Sunday school,

Sunshine Band, and Vacation Bible School. In 1960, Virginia and her late husband, Rev. Henry Griffin, co-founded the Challengers for Christ, a youth ministry. When Henry was appointed to the ministerial staff at Convent Avenue Baptist Church in the early 1960s, Virginia joined the church, became a youth leader, and a teacher of an adult class in the Sunday school. After more than 40 years at the New York City Board of Education, as teacher of children with learning disabilities, corrective reading teacher, guidance counselor, and finally as supervisor of counselors, she retired and entered a new phase of ministry. In 2000, Virginia graduated from Blanton-Peale Institute and Counseling Center and was certified as a pastoral psychotherapist. She has been counseling for 15 years and continues to teach an adult Sunday school class.

Ronald Reynard Radford, Jr. and Rhonda Radford Gray, children of Geraldine Rhoades and Ronald Reynard Radford, Sr., are the third generation of direct descendants of Sallie Anne George and Anthony Rhodes. As a business systems analyst and database architect, Ronald has traveled extensively throughout Europe, mostly in France, England, and Germany and has also spent time in the Middle East, specifically Dubai. His passion is beach volleyball. Rhonda is a project manager, certified by Project Management Institute. She is married to George Russel Gray. They have three children: Lillian Ayana, Corey Russell, and Ashley Mabel who are the fourth generation of children from the Sallie Ann George and Anthony Rhodes union. You will see Ayana's biographical statement in Chapter 16.

Corey went to the University of Arkansas, at Little Rock, to study Sports Management. Ashley, has won doubles in an Arkansas state division, but will be hanging up her tennis racquet to attend culinary school. Her sights are set on owning and operating a bakery; with her determination and work ethic, she'll make it.

Sally Ann's oldest son, Daniel McKinley Rhodes, adds to our history.

Our family is so grateful for the leadership and participation of Dan and Mabel, who are an important and special a part of our Bryant/George reunions and activities. Unfortunately, Daniel, their father, passed away when they were small. They were then raised by, their mother, Mabel Virginia Weldon Rhoades, who was to be a wonderful, caring, and religious paren. (pictured below.) It was also Addie, the sister of Daniel McKinley, who gave to her nephew Dan, the picture (featured earlier in this chapter), which confirmed for us, that these are George sisters, who are four of our earliest known ancestors.

Mabel Virginia Weldon Rhoades

Dan and Mabel (children of Daniel, Sr. and Mabel, Sr.) have been pioneers in their own rights. Mabel has contributed much in the Church arena and Dan has contributed to the music scene. (See below)

The Rhodaires, 1953: Bottom, Willie Thomas, Rev. Abraham Houston, Connie Pitts, Leon Lumpkins; Top, Willie Joyner, Danny Rhodes, Lloyd Banks

A Slave Narrative Introduces our Family Branches to Us

(Oral History Narrative)

A slaveholder on a large farm or plantation in North Carolina wanted to have a new family home built. His white field hands advised him that there was no one better than one of our relatives to accomplish his goal. This cousin of ours was the best craftsman in that community. So the slaveholder told this man, whom I will call Joe, to build his house. Joe was pleased that he had this opportunity to showcase his skills and abilities and put on his "thinking cap" in order to create a great house for his slaveholder. He planned an elaborate house that would be the envy of other nearby slaveholders.

When the house was built, it surely was a grand place and the envy of all around him. The slaveholder was so pleased that, in a moment of weakness and appreciation, he told Joe that he could build a house for his family back in the woods. Joe was overjoyed and asked his kinfolks to help him.

After some time passed, one of his white field hands asked the slaveholder if he had seen Joe's house. He answered that he had not. The inquirer felt the slaveholder should pay Joe a visit and volunteered to accompany him. When they were approaching Joe's home, the slaveholder began to get increasingly angry and by the time he arrived at Joe's house he was livid with rage.

He called to Joe to come out of his house and Joe now wondered what his slaveholder would do to him. The slaveholder cursed Joe and called him an uppity (N) and said, "I told you to build a house for your family, but I never said that you should build one just like mine." He told Joe to round up his relatives and to get off the property by sundown. It was his desire that Joe and his family would never be able to survive without proper papers and that they all would be killed. However, God's protective care for Joe and his family prevailed that night and they were able to reach Virginia and freedom.

This story has remained in our family and has been told and retold. Earl Fulcher, Dan Rhoades, and Cousin Alberta Fulcher Peterson have all claimed old Joe as their direct kin. Perhaps they all are right. Remember Cousin Geraldine shared how close and inseparable the George sisters appeared to be. This dilemma creates for us an interesting question? Could the sisters have been enslaved and lived under the rule of the same slaveholder. Was old Joe married to one of the George sisters? If this is the case, then were the other husbands the men who were involved in the building of both houses?

Cousin Fannie Fulcher Jones tells us about the Fulcher's Contributions in Their New Communities

Fannie George Fulcher was the sister of Edward George and the matriarch of the Fulchers who settled in Norfolk, Virginia. She was born in North Carolina in 1865 and had three sisters and five brothers. She and her sisters had a deep and abiding faith in the God who brought them out of enslavement. High morals, education, and family values were implanted and exhibited in her children and others whom she raised and met.

Fannie, along with her husband Columbus, who was the overseer of the Dye Trucking Farm, believed that children should receive a good sound education in school and that religion should be an integral part of the curriculum. With this belief, all of their children received their early and formal educational training at Franklinton Christian School and College in Franklinton, North Carolina, operated by Christian Churches.

Sister Fannie George Fulcher accepted the call by God to become a missionary. With the cooperation of her husband, "Mr. Columbus", as she referred to him, her daughter-in-law maintained and carried on the household responsibilities and Sister Fannie began her missionary work traveling throughout Virginia and North Carolina with the Rev. S.A. Howell, founder of the "Black Christian Churches."

Sister Fannie George Fulcher also was one of the organizers of Union Christian Church, Norfolk, Virginia. During the organizational period, the male trustees experienced some very difficult circumstances, but it was Sister Fannie who said "Men could not fulfill their destiny alone, there must be women to assist."

Very much like her brother Edward, Fannie owned and operated a hand shirt laundry in the Huntersville section of Norfolk, Virginia. She employed people who lived in Lindenwood and Huntersville Communities.

Columbus Fulcher, husband of Fannie Fulcher

James Duke Fulcher, "The Basket Man"

James Duke Fulcher was known throughout the Tide Water area and beyond as Duke the Basket Mann. Duke built his business by collecting, recycling, making baskets, bags, and other containers. He would sell them to area farmers who would use them for hauling fruits and vegetables to and from market. This was an unusual accomplishment for a Black man at that time. In 1935, he owned and operated a used container vegetable and fruit business in Norfolk, VA.

He also acquired an office and warehouse s in downtown Norfolk, VA located on Market, Main, Water, and Court Streets. Duke, as he was referred to, also was the proprietor of a fleet of five trucks and two tractor trailers. He shipped orange boxes throughout the east and west coasts via Western Railways. He exported baskets throughout Virginia, Maryland, New York, and Massachusetts. He also shipped south to North and South Carolina and Georgia. His workforce consisted of five employees along with his wife and six children.

John Fulcher was the first African Lawyer in Suffolk, VA. Due to his many contributions, "Fulcher Street" was named in his honor. After John passed, Georgia became very active at her church, St. James Episcopal. An Altar Guild has been named for her at the church. At 84, she was a Gold Medalist in the one-mile walk in the Golden Olympics held in Richmond, VA. Georgia (see picture below) celebrated her 100th birthday, August 18, 1995 in Trevose, PA.

D. R. VASQUEZ

Georgia Fulcher, right, at home with her daughter, Ernette Reid, left, is celebrating her 100th birthday on Friday, August 18. The Trevose resident will be feted at a party in her honor on Sunday, August 20 at her church, St. Andrew's in the Field Episcopal Church in Somerton.

Chapter Fourteen
Our George Family's Legacy and New Bethel Baptist Church

A Flashback to my life at New Bethel

Through the years, I kept in touch with church members and had a keen interest in the New Bethel's development and progress. It brought great joy to learn that the congregation would soon dedicate a new church building. The church home that I knew growing up would now be demolished and on the same site a new, beautiful, church constructed. I felt sincerely honored to have been asked to participate in the proposed Dedication Services which would usher in another chapter in New Bethel's history.

As a descendant of three of the founding members, I was asked to represent the eight loyal and committed Christians who accepted God's mandate and offered themselves to create a soul saving mission in the Shaw community. The 8: A.M. Worship Service, entitled: "Feeding the Multitudes" would highlight their commitment to the goals God set before them and would give recognition and honor to the leaders who led them, through generations, to victory.

The 11:00 A.M. Worship Service, Dedicatory Message would be presented by Dr. David Shannon, President of Virginia Union University. His remarks would prepare the Church congregation for their future. I was so proud of Pastor, Reverend Walter E. Fauntroy. We both grew up together at New Bethel and he has had an illustrious career for 23 years as their minister. Along with a long resume of community, political, national and international contributions, Walter was also an organizer of the famed March on Washington, and is a noted Civil Rights Leader, who worked closely with Dr. Martin Luther King, Jr.

Rhoda Bryant George and husband Edward George started our family tree after Emancipation. Edward desiring to fight for his and the freedom of his people ran away from the plantation where he was enslaved, in Jones County, and joined the Union Army. After the war and declared freedom, the couple and other family members settled initially in Craven and Pitt Counties, North Carolina. Edward served in five skirmishes, but was injured in the first, but fought on to complete his three-year commitment. They eventually became parents of 16 children. Eight, however, died due to the trials of rural life and nonexistent medical care.

Hoping to better their circumstances, the family came to Washington, D.C. and opened a laundry business. They also brought houses which they rented out to folks desiring to settle in D.C. or hoping to earn money to travel further north. Edward, because of his service related injuries, unfortunately became an invalid and passed away. Rhoda continued the laundry business and gave each of their remaining eight children down payments on a home as a wedding gift.

Rhoda was a devout Christian. She along with her son Edward and daughter Millie were founding organizers of New Bethel Baptist Church. She and other children, Edward and Millie left a great legacy for us all.

In Memoriam

Rhoda George

Founders of New Bethel Baptist Church:

    Jerry Green   Edward George

    Millie J. George   Marie Lee

    Robert Carter   David Gross

Information contributed by the Grandchildren of Rhoda and Edward George:

    Lucinda Fox Ward   Nathaniel George

    Rhoda Carrison Todd   Allen George

    Dorothea George   Foster John George

A Tribute to My Parents: Susie George Carrison and William C. Carrison

"You were my parents, who saw me as a gift from God,
You loved, nurtured, and guided me
With God's help from above.

You were my parents, who gave me a Christian Foundation.
You showed me the way, because your lives
Exemplified a Christian Spirit and love
You were my parents, who brought me up in New Bethel
Where I was a part of a true Christian community.

I was loved, I was taught, and I was guided.
It was a religious village and everyone played a part.

You were my parents, who I owe so much to,
Your sacrifice, your devotion, your love,
Will always hold many memories and much gratitude.

Your devoted daughter, Rhoda Carrison Nixon"

New Bethel's Birth and Beginning Ministry

New Bethel Baptist Church
15th Street near Fuller, N.W.
1903 - 1915

New Bethel Baptist Church
9th and S Streets, N.W.
1915 - 1977

Chapter 1: The Beginning (1803 – 1940)

New Bethel's first pastor was Reverend Dr. William D. Jarvis. Under His pastorate the church experienced spiritual growth and prosperity during his 37 years of Leadership. On February 7, 1915, the New Bethel congregation held its first worship service at a site located on 9th and S Streets, N.W. Rev. Jarvis retired leaving a rich legacy as a benchmark for Christian outreach and service.

Annie George was a Deaconess and Edward George a Church Founder

Chapter 2 (1941 – 1958)

Reverend C. David Foster assumed the pastorate of New Bethel in 1941. Under Rev. Foster, the church name was changed to Greater New Bethel Baptist Church and many clubs and auxiliaries were established to meet the needs of the church and community. Like his predecessor, Rev. Foster oversaw continued spiritual and numerical growth and prosperity during his tenure. Rev. Foster succumbed to illness in 1958.

Aunt Millie (Founding Member) and Rev. Foster

Chapter 3: Casting the Net (1959 – 2009)

Reverend Walter E. Fauntroy, a son of New Bethel was selected to serve as Supply Pastor shortly after the death of Reverend Foster. In 1959, the church unanimously voted to name Rev Fauntroy as the third pastor of New Bethel. The church was renamed Greater New Bethel Baptist Church and a new era of Christian service in the Shaw community was born. Under Rev Fauntroy's leadership, both New Bethel and the Shaw community were revitalized. The New Bethel Housing Corporation was formed in 1958 and in 1973, the

Foster House Apartment building was constructed on the corner of 9th Street and Rhode Island Avenue N.W. This 76-unit complex continues to be a corner stone within the community as it provides housing to low and moderate income residents in Shaw. Additionally, New Bethel was at the forefront of significant change locally and nationwide during Rev. Fauntroy's tenure. This includes the design and implementation of the Shaw Urban Renewal Project, engagement in civil and voting rights campaigns with Martin Luther King, Jr., the effort to win Home Rule for residents of the District of Columbia, and numerous worldwide humanitarian campaigns during Rev. Fauntroy's tenure as a member of the United States House of Representatives.

It started at New Bethel, Lifetime Best Friends:

Florence Watson Jackson
Edna Watson Owens
Rhoda Carrison Nixon

Sermon presented by Sister Rhoda Todd (now Nixon) and introduced by Sister Florence W. Jackson..

"The Lord done great things for us, whereof we are glad." Psalms 126:3

8:00 A.M. Worship Service

Presiding: Reverend James H. Jones, Assistant Pastor

Introduction of Speaker	Sister Rhoda Todd
Sister Florence W. Jackson	Descendant of the Founder

"FEEDING THE MULTITUDES"

(1902 – 1982)

It is twilight beside the Sea of Galilee. As the sun slips below the horizon, common greyness, silvers everything. Jesus, leading the inner circle of his friends, has not been able to escape the multitudes of troubled and hurting people. The crowds have followed them into the remote campsite and have stayed with them throughout the heat of the afternoon.

Now it is evening. The shadows have lengthened across the hills and the inward greyness of spirit descends over the twelve disciples. They now sit in mark contrast to the multiple shades of twilight.

Simon, Andrew, James, John, Peter and the others are full of anger. They are tired of answering the same questions; they are worn from the countless demands of the crowds: the blind, the handicapped, the troubled, and the rich in wealth but poor in spirit. They are tired of those who doubt that Jesus is our Savior and the hour is late.

New Bethel, it is from the type setting that our faith was born. It was from this beginning that our journey with Jesus, our Christ, laid its foundation. Four stages mark our faith journey; four stages mark the site where we established our church. The place we claimed to live out Christ's mission here on earth.

Jesus came to give us the opportunity of renewal. As we see the death of one stage of life, we always see the resurrection and birth of a new and challenging phase. We can feel spent by the greyness of the twilight, but we can be renewed by the dawn. Today marks the dawn, New Bethel, of a new day. This will be a new time of challenge and opportunity, a new day of mission and of hope, a new day of blessing and of grace.

Our scene has shifted from centuries ago. The disciples are no longer Simon, Andrew, James, John and Peter, but New Bethel's founders and the year is 1902. The disciples are now brother Jerry Green, Robert Carter, David, Gross, Edward George and sisters Rhoda George, Marie Lee, and Millie J. George. The mission is no longer the remote campsite in Galilee, But New Bethel Baptist Church on Meridian Hill.

I can still remember, as a child, seeing my mother's face alive with excitement as she recalled the earlier days in the church on the Hill under the pastorate of Rev. William Jarvis. She rejoiced as she remembered her relationship to many of the members. It was for her an extended family, a support community. She also recalled some of sad moments and the loss of family, friends, and members who have gone to reap their reward with our god.

The church on the Hill grew and prospered. The Meridian Hill Community viewed New Bethel as a Beacon of light in the port. It was the constant in the storm. After 13 years, New Bethel could no longer be contained in their original church on the Hill. It was time to seek a new and larger campsite. It was now time to enter a new phase. The third stage was upon us.

On February 7, 1913, the cast of characters changed from the founders of 1902 to the new leaders who would pioneer and meet the challenges of the new era. It was the dawning of a glorious day for Deacon Edward Brent, Mrs. Henrietta Epps, Mrs. Bertha Peyton and Miss. G. E. Jones. There were so many others who could be mentioned, because without them, we could not really tell the story of New Bethel's history. We could not describe the faith journey; we could not tell how it fed the multitudes.

Under the pastorate of Reverend Jarvis, whose wife was a cousin of mine on my father's side, I surrendered my life to the cause of Jesus Christ. Like the disciples of old, I wanted to follow Jesus. I also wanted to follow in the footsteps of my grandmother, Rhoda George; my aunt Millie Carter; and my uncle, Edward George.

I wanted to feed the multitudes like the mentors of my childhood: Henrietta Epps, G. E. Jones, Elsie Piper, and there is one I would like to highlight, who was very important to all of us, Mr. Birdell C. Whitfield, our Youth Advisor and Superintendent of our Sunday School. Although, I surrendered my life to Christ, my Service of Baptism was delayed until my mother could be present. My mother was in the hospital at that time.

On Mother's Day, May 1941, the first Sunday of Reverend C. David Foster's pastorate with us, I again walked up to join New Bethel, this time accompanied by Roberta Bryant (Jenkins) my cousin. Both mothers had been ill and now were able to be present to witness our baptism and our induction into the membership of New Bethel Baptist Church. What a day of rejoicing that was for all of us.

I grew up and moved to New York City to live. Many times I have looked back to review my religious roots here in New Bethel. These child hood reflections have brought anew-the joys, some sad moments, the mission and the wonderful spirit of the folks of New Bethel. I have often shared these experiences with my children, Gerald and JoAnne, who are now grown with children of their own. But I wanted them to know my religious beginnings and how those experiences have influenced and shaped, through -out my life, my faith journey with my Lord and Savior Jesus Christ.

Today a new chapter is being launched in New Bethel's history. Today's dawn ushers in a new era. Under the leadership of your present pastor, the Reverend Walter E. Fauntroy, you have reached another milestone, a fourth stage in your history. You will now dedicate a new building, a new campsite for the church family and the Shaw community. The Lord can truly be proud of your gift to the Glory His Kingdom. You can now extend and give more services to feed the multitudes around you.

I feel privileged to represent the founders of the past and wish to salute two persons whose lives and contributions have spanned several periods in our history: Mrs. Bertha Peyton, who joined New Bethel in 1909 and Mrs. Virginia Leonard who joined in 1913. We are so grateful that they are still with us today.

I join you in being proud of our predecessors who felt the call of mission from our Lord, Jesus Christ, and joined with others to charter our church, New Bethel Baptist. Ours is a wonderful history, rich in love, dedication, tenacity and service. The founders were the standard bearers. They had a vision that a church could be a dynamic force to meet the needs of people through the ages. You have now proudly joined their struggle and joy. You now look forward to a brilliant future, one which will be a beacon of power in the Lord's name for years to come.

All through the seasons of sowing and reaping.
All through the harvest of song and tears
Hold us close in your tender keeping
O Maker of all New Years.

Written and presented by Rhoda C Todd, descendant of three Charter Members of New Bethel Baptist Church, November 28, 1982.

Sister Rhoda Todd and Reverend Walter E. Fauntroy

Chapter Fifteen
The Bryant Family Pays Tribute to Our Achieving and Accomplished Adults

We are proud of our adult family members who are among today's leaders and making their mark in the many areas of national and international life.

Special Tribute to David Botts

David Botts is the son of Barbara and John (Johnny) Botts, grandson of Alma Carrison Botts and John Botts, and great-nephew to author, Rhoda Nixon. During his early years, David faced many challenges. Although he appeared to develop normally for the first 2½ years of his life, he evidenced an absence of verbal skills. David was eventually diagnosed as having Autism Spectrum Disorder, commonly known as Asperger's Syndrome. Specialist advised his parents that David might never develop normal speech and language, and during early childhood he exhibited many of the classic symptoms of this disorder.

By the time David reached seventh grade, and because of the help he had received from loving and understanding parents and former teachers, he was placed in a regular classroom setting. When David graduated from high school, he received the prestigious "Youth Achievement Award" from a local county executive.

After graduating from high school, David first received an Associate's degree and then went on to receive a Bachelor of Arts Degree in Business Administration. This level of success was unthinkable after his childhood diagnosis.

David is currently a movie theater usher who interacts with hundreds of people on a regular basis, an occupation that was unthinkable when he was diagnosed with autism. David started at the theater as a volunteer, but was such a hit with regular patrons that management offered him a permanent position. He is very active in his church and has an important role in its Young Adult group. David has been selected to research venues for the church's special activities. He has an outgoing, friendly personality, and is loved and respected by people who know him.

David has greatly enjoyed our family reunions. Our family has watched David grow up before our eyes, and he has always been supported with loving, encouraging, and patient parents. We offer to you, Barbara and Johnnie, our heartfelt appreciation for our family member. You are winners, too. God gave David the right parents to raise this very special son. Our Bryant/George accolades go out to you.

David's story shows that there is hope for all of us who face serious challenges, and some of us face more than others. David is truly a success story. It is Johnny and Barbara's desire and prayer that David's story will give hope to others who are facing challenges they feel are insurmountable. They urge you not to give up, because with a persevering and God-filled spirit you can, as David did, achieve success.

JoAnne Stanback

Groundbreaking Medical Researcher, Leader, Author, and Co-Coordinator of the Bryant/George Family

JoAnne Berry Stanback is the daughter of Rhoda C. Nixon and George Edwin Berry (deceased). Her greatest treasure and achievement in life has been to be the Mom of three extraordinary, dynamic children: Michele, Matthew, and Michael Stanback. She says, "They truly have been my inspiration, motivation and complete joy, and they propel me to move forward." In addition to motherhood, JoAnne has experienced several rewarding professions in life: Medical Researcher, Director of Subject Recruitment for Department of Defense's Chronic Pain and Fatigue Research Center, Interior Designer (designing over 25 homes in the DMV vicinity), and a Volunteer Coordinator at a Public Charter School where she governed over 206 volunteers yearly.

JoAnne's most memorable professional career highlight was when she independently ran two Cyclical Mastalgia (CM) Protocols for the Chief of Surgical Oncology at Walter Reed Medical Center and the Associate Professor at Uniform Services University of Health Sciences, Department of Psychiatry. In 1998, the double-blind, placebo-controlled multicenter study was developed to investigate the safety and efficacy of Efamast (gamolenic acid), with or without antioxidant vitamins and minerals, in the management of moderate to severe benign breast pain (mastalgia). JoAnne initiated and connected the protocol to Sun Laboratories. This lead to the project's partnership with Scotia Pharmaceuticals and the acquisition of the

Efamast capsules for their study. This was the first time in America's history that the Department of Defense had an intercontinental study with Britain that compared the effects of evening primrose oil on cycling breast pain. Also in 1995, she received co-authorship after analyzing over 250 abstracts for the article: "Sex, Race, and Topic in Behavioral Medicine Research: An Analysis of the 1995 Society of Behavioral Medicine (SBM) Scientific Sessions, Deborah N. Ader, Ph.D., Tracy Sboracco, Ph.D., JoAnne Stanback, B.S. and Loretta L. Gallant, B.A. Annals of Behavioral Medicine 19 (Suppl.), S1-S224".

On a personal note, in 2012, JoAnne documented our family history in two volumes from the mid 1800's to 2012 for the July 20–22nd, 2012 family reunion. She connected our family branches by soliciting interviews, chronicling facts, linking each person to our family tree, and formulating an eighty-page family historical resource.

In 2015, JoAnne accepted the baton to become the next successor as the Bryant/George Family Co–Coordinator, along with her nephew, Albert Debnam. She presently manages our family web page where eighty-one family members have accepted an invitation to participate. Close to forty-five members follow our successes, birthdays, anniversaries, graduations, and prayers every week. Our connection range is vast, with family members residing in Liberia, Canada, and throughout the United States. JoAnne has been faithfully committed and has shown steadfast loyalty to our family as she continues to keep our ties anchored via social media technology.

Roland Bryant Jr.
Multifaceted Artisan and Businessman

Roland Bryant is a great-grandson of Noah Bryant, who was one of our earliest recorded ancestors. Roland is a gifted artist, an electrical engineer of great stature, and now has started his own business in Video and Film production.

At an early age, Roland became intrigued with art and was an active participant in art programs at schools he attended. He created murals that covered school walls and posters that were used for Cub Scout and Boy Scout troop meetings. While in junior high, he received a Kodak Super 8 sound movie camera from his dad. It was a gift he had always longed for. He instantly became known as the neighborhood producer of karate movies. In high school, Roland aspired to become a medical illustrator and studied anatomy and physiology. He also planned to attend Pratt Institute with a focus on creating anatomical illustrations.

However, Roland elected to put his desire to attend Pratt on hold in order to help his family in their electrical contracting business. Roland would represent the third generation to pursue this noble profession. Since this was expected of him, and also because Roland felt proud of his family's leadership in this area, he agreed to join them in their business venture. So immediately following high school, he enrolled in Detroit's International Brotherhood of Electrical Workers' (IBEW) apprenticeship program where he studied and worked for four years. He also studied architectural drawing and drafting at Wayne County Community College.

Although Roland worked in the electrical industry, he remained drawn to art. During his years as an apprentice electrician, he enrolled at the Center for Creative Studies where he studied commercial art and the art of prospective and proportions. At CCS, he was able to learn the technical side of the art he truly loved.

After some time, Roland moved to California where he started his own electrical contracting company. By age twenty-nine, he had earned his first state license as Master Electrician and Contractor. His company, Bryant Electric Company (of California), received its first contract to complete work on the Culver City Courthouse. Other significant projects were then granted to his company: University of California's 5,000 volt staging system, electrical upgrades for the Los Angeles Unified School District, and work for the U.S. Marshals Service offices. One project that brought Roland considerable gratification was the electrical installation at the Radiology Oncology department for Los Angeles University Medical Center. The installation at the department included installing linear accelerators and beta Tron machines, which are used to externally focus radiation on a cancer site.

Life changes took Roland back to his hometown of Detroit where he continued his career as an electrical contractor and earned another state license. After thirty-six years in the electrical industry, Roland recognized that he had never transitioned into a calling which involved his passion for art.

Then one day, during the early days of computer video streaming, Roland had a breakthrough and decided to start a small business that included filming local bands and streaming their sessions to the Internet. This new venture earned him a first copyright and an open door to the film industry. Through his video work, he has met and worked with several film students and professionals.

Regardless of the job, Roland believes that everyone should strive to be the best at their craft. In between film projects, he now works at honing his post-production skills by studying at Screenwriters University. He also feels his willingness to remain a student makes his contribution to film projects invaluable. Roland's lifelong passion for art has also led him to produce a full feature movie that was nationally distributed and short films that have become award-winning at film festivals.

Wain Jenkins
Our Bryant/Jenkins Artisan

Wain, the nephew of Roberta Bryant Jenkins and Leonard Jenkins, is a gifted and multifaceted artist. Our cousin, Wain, graduated from Calvin Coolidge High School, one of the best local high schools in Washington, D.C. He received a Bachelor of Architecture degree from a prestigious local university.

After practicing architecture for a few years, Wain became interested in construction management and has spent the last thirty years as a Certified Construction Manager (CCM) for an international company. After some time, he also decided to rekindle male modeling, a pursuit he enjoyed in high school and college.

In 2009, Wain auditioned for the Washington National Opera and landed a role as the Crap Shooter in "Porgy and Bess" at the John F. Kennedy Center Opera House. Performing on the big stage in front of 2,000 people seemed natural for him. Since then, his acting/modeling career has led him to more roles at the Kennedy Center, including "Tosca", "Force of Destiny", "La Boheme", "Iphigenie en Tauride" (with Placido Domingo), and "Appomattox."

Wain has also played in "The Nutcracker" and "Cinderella" with the Classical Ballet Theater. Some of his other accomplishments include the plays "Take Me Out" at the Gunston Theater, "Sins of the Father", "Do Drop In", and as Doaker in "The Piano Lesson" at The Publick Playhouse, and performances in "Am I My Brother's Keeper" in Maryland and Georgia.

Our artisan has performed in supporting roles in the following films: "The Touchstone" and "The Infinite," and in background in "Creed" with Sylvester Stallone and Michael B Jordan. He recently filmed with Danny Glover and Gabrielle Union in "Almost Christmas."

Wain has appeared in commercials for Medstar Health, Carolina Kitchen, Capital One, Adidas (Coach for RG3 in "What Light Does"), Harley Davidson, Trusted Health Plan, Home Depot, Peter T Nichol, and Dominion Power, to name a few. He can also be seen in a principle role in the music video, "Cried My Last Tear" for R/B Artist Debbie Poole and featured background in the television shows "House of Cards" on Netflicks, "Veep" on HBO, and "Nightmare Next-door," "Evil Kin," "Deadly Affairs," and "Who the Bleep Did I Marry" for ID Discovery and "For My Man" for TV One.

Wain models in the prestigious "Fashion on the Hudson" in New York City, Atlanta and Philadelphia, and along with his designer business partner, produces "Fashion at the Mansion" in Mitchellville, MD each year, which raises money for charities such as The United Way.

This year, Wain will be touring in a three-man play, "Black Men's Truth/White Man's Burden" and also is appearing in the spring and fall as Henry Johnson in the stage play "Snap Honey." He will also portray a pastor in the web series "House of Sharkes."

Although his acting and modeling career have taken off, Wain continues to work as a construction manager and enjoys life with his wife, daughter, and his son-in-law.

Gerald D. Smith Chemist
Organizational Director and Lecturer

Gerald was born in Harlem Hospital in New York City. He attended school in New York City and Washington, DC. Following graduation from the Peter Stuyvesant High School (a special science preparatory high school), he entered Howard University in its centennial class (1963-1967). Graduating from the university with a major in chemistry and a minor in mathematics, Gerald began his career in the public health field, working in various capacities at the Walter Reed Army Medical Center (clinical chemist) and in the Maryland Health Department System (food and water chemist).

In 1971, Gerald returned to Walter Reed Army Institute of Research where he accepted a research position in the Department of Endocrinology & Metabolism. In this capacity, he was highly commended for his contribution to hormone research and the computerization of data production and data evaluation relative to hormone research.

In 1978, Gerald accepted a position as the first International Executive Director of the Phi Beta Sigma Fraternity, Inc., an international African-American collegiate organization; an appointment he filled for twelve years. He was widely traveled as an organizer and lecturer with an emphasis on organizational development and parliamentary procedure. During the 1990 calendar year, he served as the executive assistant (temporary) to the CEO of Almic Broadcasting, Inc. (now trading as Radio One, TV One and Syndication One), as a business consultant, lecturer, writer, and radio personality.

Gerald currently lectures on Afrocentricity; Decoding Societal Racism/White Supremacy Behavior; Bridging Philosophical & Cultural; Organizational Management and Development; Construction of Organizational Constitutions and Parliamentary Procedure. In addition to his lecture responsibilities, Gerald worked as an Assistant Editor for a publishing firm and directs *The African Renaissance Institute* (a think tank and presentational vehicle).

Gerald is the son of attorney, Lawrence Smith (now deceased), and our author, Rev. Rhoda Nixon. Gerald and his wife, Lynette, have been married for 47 years and are parents of Jason C.E. Smith (Monica) and Steven L.L. Smith (April Yvette) and they are proud grandparents of Najia, Kameron, and Christian Smith. Gerald is the great-grandson of Rhoda and Edward Dudley George and is named "Dudley" in honor of his great-grandfather.

Memoirs of the Botts family

When William Botts, affectionately known as "Billy," met a young, Northeastern University nursing student, named Emma Rose Saunders, the Botts family began a journey that continued when they married in New York City in 1968.

Billy was a bright and respectful young man from the Bronx, New York. A former track athlete in high school, he so excelled academically that he qualified as an enrollee at Columbia University. At Columbia, Billy also excelled as a member of the row team.

He has a twin brother, Johnny, both of whom were products of a very demanding upbringing. The brothers grew up loyal to their parents. When faced with a difficult decision, the Botts brothers put their lives on hold to care for their ailing parents. This was no surprise. The "Botts Boys" were always there for family. This trait would inherently be passed down to generations to come.

Emma Rose Botts was born in New York City during the heightened climate of racial segregation. Despite her struggles as a black woman, she was awarded an academic scholarship to attend Northeastern University in Boston, MA, where she studied nursing.

Bill would visit her frequently on the weekends during his time at Columbia. As time went on, he had to attend to his ailing mother and take a break from school. Yet, Emma Rose remained a constant positive influence in his life. They eventually married in 1968 in New York City.

Emma Rose would become the "rock" of our family. She was my hero. Professionally, her expertise in nursing carried her throughout many disciplines. She began as a pediatric nurse at Flower Hospital in Manhattan and quickly became the head nurse in that department. The family grew and moved to upstate New York where she worked as a director in the human services field at different agencies. Caring for individuals was in her blood. It was a trait that would undoubtedly be passed down to me.

I have worked in the field of human services for over twenty years. My years spent working on the front line of care made me a stronger, compassionate, and much more patient person. Working with individuals with intellectual disabilities takes a special soul with a kind heart. Today, I live in Allentown, PA. I have a B.A. in Intercultural Studies from East Stroudsburg University, and continue the tradition of caring by working on the management level in the human services field.

Walter, my younger brother, is the hardest working man I know. Finding his path early in life, he became a mechanic shortly out of high school. He worked his way up the ranks in the automotive business becoming a Head Technician at the Subaru Company. Walter currently lives in Monroe, New York with his fiancé, Susan Grimes, and their beautiful daughter, Cecelia.

As parents and grandparents, we marvel as we witness our offspring flourish in anything they attempt. Sometimes they fail. Sometimes they succeed.

Nevertheless, we are always proud to see things in them that they themselves would never notice. This was the case during two defining events that underscore the possibilities of these young adults in our family.

The date was March 6, 2016. Cecelia had her very first photo shoot as a model. She was quiet but nervous. She was also confident. We watched her move around in front of the many photographers jockeying for positioning. They were seeking that perfect, necessary shot. They directed her to move around from pose to pose. She did so with an effortless flow. Strange for her at first, but then it became natural. She was encouraged by the other older, more experienced models. It empowered her! "Those eyes," said one photographer. "My goodness, she's beautiful." We always wondered what would be the one thing that Cece could excel at beyond any doubt. I thought to myself, this is it. She is also an inquisitive young lady who has loved riding horses....and yes, even helped her dad fix cars. But then I saw it. She smiled an honest, unsolicited smile. That's when we knew. I looked at her parents, Walter and Susan. He was smiling from ear-to-ear, and she was crying. They saw it too.

My son, Donte, also constantly amazes me. How often does a father say that about his own son? Well, it is true. He has overcome so much in his eighteen years. He suffered through a severe speech impediment, diagnosis of learning disabled, and a product of a bitter divorce and custody battle. He overcame all of this alone before the age of twelve, and without counseling or another sibling to lean on. Donte has played the piano, earned a black belt in Taekwondo, and became a very good high school student. For me, his defining moment came while playing football. As a junior, he was awarded 2nd Team All-Conference and Honorable Mention All-Area. Despite being injured for his entire senior season, he never missed a start. His efforts landed him an athletic scholarship to Marist College. He is currently in his sophomore year majoring in Sports Communication.

Our family has always understood that hard work pays off. That mind set has and will continue to be passed on for generations to come.

Memoirs were written by Michael Botts, grandson of Alma Carrison Botts, and John Botts. Alma is the sister of our Author, Rhoda Carrison Nixon.

Ronda Bryant
A Multifaceted Achiever

Ronda Bryant, born July 22nd, 1959 in Detroit, Michigan, is the oldest child of Roland Bryant and Violet Kakuno Bryant and the great-great-granddaughter of Noah Bryant, one of our earliest ancestors. She grew up in Detroit with her brother Roland Bryant Jr.; both are of African-American and Japanese descent.

Ronda has overcome great odds. Growing up in the 1960s, a decade when African-Americans were brutally confronted with racism, Ronda experienced racist attacks by Caucasians as well as African-Americans. During the sixties, civil differences in Detroit were evident in schools. Although Ronda's elementary schools were integrated, the classrooms were not. Blacks were in a separate class labeled "slow," while most of the whites were in another room and considered "advanced." Ronda was in the class deemed "slow," and she began to believe that she was a slow learner.

It was not until Ronda's parents transferred her to Epiphany Catholic School where she tested in the upper 95th percentile that she was immediately admitted to the advanced class. In mathematics, she was at the head of the class and was allowed to teach herself. Her confidence began to increase only to fall again when she started high school and was told by her white counselor that she should take home economics. Her high school counselor added that she was not "college material." After the counselor's comments, Ronda stopped coming to class, only attending school on test days. She received a below-average GPA during this time.

While some would have distanced themselves from both ethnic groups, Ronda developed a broader perspective about society and social problems. She attended Frank Cody High School where she developed a better understanding of the world's segregating behavior and graduated at age 16. She left school to travel with Up with People (UOP), an educational organization whose stated mission was to bridge cultural barriers and create global understanding through service and a musical show. She joined the organization for the 1976 World Tour where she performed three 1-hour specials for Tele Visa in Mexico as the principal vocalist.

It is in Mexico that she met Anthony Quinn, an actor, who was also on the board of UOP. In 1976, she stayed with host families throughout the United States, which allowed her to broaden her insight and her cultural/ethnic tolerance that she now lives by. During the 1976 tour, she was able to perform for two presidents, Gerald Ford and Jimmy Carter, and at various state fairs, universities, small towns, and larger urban cities.

However, her greatest achievement was the opportunity to meet and develop friendships with her host families from all walks of life — southern whites, upper class elites, middle class, and American-natives on Indian reservations.

After leaving UOP, Ronda moved to New York City to attend The Julliard School of Music. It was there that she met and married an Italian man from Naples. Their marriage produced her only child, Francesco. Soon after his birth, the couple divorced, and Ronda became a single mother. During Francesco's adolescence, Ronda joined her father to start an electrical construction company called Basil Electric Inc. Both father and daughter started with just a few expanded projects for governmental agencies. During that time, Ronda, wanting to expand her knowledge, enrolled in the engineering program at Wayne State University where she held a 4.0 GPA and was on the Dean's list every semester. Remembering her high school counselor's statement that she was not "college material," Ronda surpassed even her own expectations.

However, as times changed with an economic recession, Ronda's career path pivoted to a nursing program. After watching multiple engineering and construction companies collapse, she decided that nursing was a safer choice for her because she needed to take care of her family. She left Wayne State University and transferred to Madonna University's nursing department. She subsequently received her BS degree in nursing, and graduated Summa Cum Laude. She began her nursing career at John Dingell Veteran Hospital as a registered nurse and later as an intensive care nurse at Sinai-Grace Hospital. During her employment at Sinai-Grace, she received her master's degree from their nurse-practitioner program.

As a nurse-practitioner, she worked at Harper Hospital on the surgical intensive team in cardiac surgery for three years. She left Harper to work for the Michigan Department Correctional Department as a medical provider. There, she developed a successful diabetic program for inmates that resulted in 80% of diabetics having an A1C level below 7%.

However, her greatest success has been her son, Francesco, and she has focused much of her time on raising him. Francesco, who was diagnosed with ADHD, also encountered some difficulty in school. He eventually scored 147 on an IQ test and won two city science awards. At the age of 10, Francesco was invited to join the Environmental Committee in the city of Dearborn, after he had won the Dearborn Science Award for his project on recyclable materials.

Ronda always emphasized the importance of education and successfully instilled in Francesco the confidence to attend college. He currently has a BS degree in Engineering Computer Science and is now working on his master's degree. His mother Ronda is planning to pursue a doctoral degree.

Frank L. Wilson Jr.
Musician-Drummer-Songwriter and Teacher

Frank is a great-grandson of Fannie George, one of our earliest known ancestors. Frank has become the drummer of choice for studio work, club dates, tours, and clinics. During his tenure, he played with legendary jazz organist, Jimmy Smith. Frank has played all the major clubs from New York's Blue Note to Emeryville's Kimball's East. No stranger on the tour circuit, Frank has played in Poland, Russia, West Germany, France, Switzerland, Italy, Bermuda and Japan. Over the years Frank has developed a reputation as a sensitive and reliable performer, backing up singers, musicians, and performers including, Jon Hendricks, Les McCann, Dave Benoit, Eddie "Clean-Head" Vinson, Joe Liggins and The Honeydrippers, John Mayall, Linda Hopkins, and many more artists.

Frank has performed in many feature films, television, and theater as an actor. He has also done side work as a drummer-musician in the following:

>Miss Lonely Hearts- Masterpiece Theatre-Feat
>Am gonna Get You Sucka- Feature
>Dead Again- Feature
>Arsenio Hall Show- Television
>Seinfeld- Television
>Picket Fence- Television
>E.R. – Television

Sitting down with Frank was such a joy. He is very open and talks from the hip. You will enjoy listening to an interview about his travels with the music he loves. The interview was recorded September 25, 2013, at local 47 in Hollywood CA. Check it out:

Night Journey Rewind with Drummer Frank L. Wilson at (http://www.nightjourneyrewind.com/home/night journey-with drummer-frank wilson, jr.).

Chapter Sixteen

Our Ancestors' Legacy is in Good Hands

Our Young People hold the Bryant/George Banner High

When we look back at our many family reunions, it seems as if it was just yesterday when we started those wonderful celebrations. We also cannot fully grasp that our young people have grown up in front of our eyes. They are now competent, young men and women who are achieving so much in their respective careers and lives. Our reunions have truly been a village that helped to raise them. Along with their parents, we also have been a source of encouragement, training, love, and support.

Through the years, our reunions have included programs and activities geared toward the development of our young people. These reunions provided an arena where our youngsters could explore new ideas, begin to discover their interests, abilities, and develop meaningful relationships.

Now, we the Bryant/George supporters have the joy of seeing the growth of our young people come to full bloom. We now have young adults who are products of the many life and societal changes that have occurred, as well as the high technological advances that currently bombard and challenge our lives. As this evolution took place, our young people were also evolving. Now they are equipped to take their place in this new phase of life that often leaves us oldsters behind.

On the following pages are examples of how some of our girls and boys have grown and flourished in our Bryant/George "laboratory." Featured are biographical sketches of some of our younger family members, now grown up, as well as new young adults who have more recently joined our reunions.

Presentations for Awards and Special Recognition

Our Topic

"What Family Means To Me"

Johnnetta Fulcher Brown

Michele Stanback

Tysha Tolbert

Robert Tolbert

Matthew Stanback

Pictures: George/Bryant Family Reunion
The Doubletree Inn Hotel
Norfolk, Virginia
July 1996

Our Bryant/George Young Adults Biographical Portraits

Lillian Ayana Gray
Writer, Published Researcher, and Artist

A passionate writer, Lillian Ayana Gray (or Ayana as most call her) is the oldest child of Rhonda Radford Gray and George Russel Gray. She is a fourth generation descendant of Sally Ann George, one of our earliest George ancestors. Always an outstanding student, Ayana became a published author during her senior year in high school. Her research paper, "Sex-Selective Abortion, Female Infanticide, and Their Lasting Effects in China and India" was published in The Concord Review, the only academic journal in the world that accepts papers from high school students across the United States as well as 44 other countries. Ayana was the recipient of the annual Emerson prize of $1,000 given to writers of the best essays in the journals for a given year.

Ayana is not only a writer but a talented artist who has won prizes for art work throughout high school. As a lark, she entered a contest to win tickets to the Belmont Race in 2015, and her drawing of American Pharaoh won her two seats at the race. Mother and daughter were witnesses to a bit of horse racing history when he won the Triple Crown.

She received her Bachelor of Arts degree in both Political Science and African and African-American Studies *cum laude* from the University of Arkansas at Fayetteville in May 2015. While at University, she was initiated into the Kappa Iota Chapter of Alpha Kappa Alpha Sorority, Incorporated and served as its president for two terms.

Following graduation, she received an offer of employment from her alma mater to serve in its Office of Development Research as an analyst. Ayana plans to begin pursuit of a Master of Arts in History beginning in fall 2016 and will subsequently pursue a Doctor of Philosophy degree in History. Ultimately, she aims to become a university professor.

Michele Lisa Stanback

Artist, Educator, and Eco-womanist

Michele is an artist, art therapist, and an educator of ten years. Infusing the arts, Michele enjoys exploring rituals, and breathing new life into sacred spaces for meaningful reflection. While obtaining her M.Div. at Union Theological Seminary in the City of New York, she utilized her unique lens and framework to illuminate issues in Social Ethics, Ecofeminism and Indigenous wisdom to inform sustainable practices through the arts—seeking ethical approaches to Mother Earth.

In her position as Student Fellow in the newly developed Center for Earth Ethics at Union Theological Seminary, she had the honor of collaborating with multi-faith and Native American leaders seeking to change public consciousness in a way that will lead to the changes in policy and culture that are necessary to prevent climate change and inequity from getting worse.

Michele is a founding member of the Yes and Ministry, a community of multi-faith people who gather to worship through creative engagement, improvisation, and collaboration. This fall, she will complete an internship with Intersections International, *"uniting art and community to transform conflicts through original theatrical works, collective creativity, and leadership development for underserved populations."*

Honing her current research in investigating stories and myth-making, creating new consciousness or cosmology, as ways of reconnecting women of color to Mother Earth, she has had the honor to present at several conferences including: The World Youth Right to Dialogue Conference in Trieste, Italy; Landscaping Change Conference in Bath Spa, London; Mid-Atlantic AAR; International Society of Religion, Nature and Culture; The Youth Summit with UPROSE; and the World Student Christian Federation Leadership Conference.

Michele has a B.A. in Individualized Studies from University of Maryland, College Park, and a MPS in Creative Arts Therapy and Creativity Development from Pratt Institute in New York City.

Tysha Tolbert

Multi-Faceted Trailblazer: Computer Scientist Engineer, Business Woman

Tysha Clarise Tolbert is the middle child and only daughter of Clarise (Gibson) Tolbert and Edward Briggford Tolbert. She is also the great, great granddaughter of Robert George, one of our earliest George ancestors.

Tysha is a decorated National Merit Scholar and graduated from high school with additional honors. During high school, she was also a competitive athlete, earning local rankings in track and field as well as cheerleading.

In college, she was an active member of the National Society of Black Engineers, which strives to "increase the number of culturally responsible Black engineers who excel academically, succeed professionally, and positively impact the community." Upon graduation, she was awarded the School of Engineering and Applied Science award for University Impact and Community Service. Tysha's commitment to the growth and development of young people is commendable. She mentors over twenty college students, recent college graduates, and several minorities and young women in the IT field.

Tysha received a Bachelor of Arts degree in Computer Science. She also obtained several IT and sales certifications which only made her more marketable in her area of expertise. She earned certifications as a Sales Expert, Certified Network Professional, and a Certified Network Design Professional. She has also been recognized as an Accredited Sales Professional in Networking and Security and a Certified Sales Professional. These certificates have enabled Tysha to have notable success in sales, business consulting, sales engineering, and business development.

Kismet Sofia Debnam
Our Artist of Illustration and Painting

Kismet Debnam, eldest daughter of Albert and Jaana Debnam, is the great granddaughter of Albert Nixon and Rhoda C. Nixon. Kismet lived with her family in Finland for 6 years.

In 2005/2006, while in elementary school, Kismet played the violin in 5th and 6th grade. In high school, she joined the Photography Club. She was admitted to a special program for high school students on the campus of Yale University where she continued her study of photography and added videography, printmaking, and sculpture.

Kismet later attended an arts college in the United States, majoring in illustration and painting. While in college, she worked as a library assistant and interned at a prestigious gallery. She also did live paintings, attended auction events, and also worked as an usher and art handler. During her junior year, she studied art abroad in Italy for a summer. She graduated with a Bachelor of Fine Arts degree.

Kismet had her first gallery showing of her works in Massachusetts in 2016 and is contemplating her next professional endeavors.

Elizabeth Wateh Gray
Teacher, International Christian Educator and Missionary

Elizabeth Gray is affectionately called Lizzie by family and friends. Her middle name, Wateh, so descriptive of her, means peace. She is also the great, great, great granddaughter of Robert George, one of our earliest known enslaved ancestors. Robert George, after being freed, pursued a better life through the Marcus Garvey Back to Africa Movement and settled in Liberia, West Africa. Her parents, although born in Liberia, when war broke out, were forced to flee to London, England, where Lizzie was born. The family came to the United States when she was about two years old.

Lizzie received a Bachelor's degree and certifications in three areas: Elementary Education, Early Childhood Education, and English as a Second Language (ESOL).

Currently, Lizzie is a 5th grade teacher, an accomplished creative dancer, and founder of an ensemble formed with two classmates. They were featured, with great acclaim, at our 2012 family reunion.

Elizabeth is also passionate about the Lord, and she spends a lot of her time ministering and praying for the lost and helping those in need. This summer, she had her first international mission trip to Japan where she sought to be an instrument of God's love to their children, as she glorified His name. When Elizabeth is not teaching, she is usually spending time with family, having fellowship with brothers and sisters in the Lord, or traveling locally and internationally.

Percy Caldwell
Global Account Manager, Belden Inc.
Community Organizer and Leader

Percy Caldwell, son of Ronita Jones Caldwell and Percy Caldwell, called "Trey" by family and friends, is the great-great-grandson of Jane Bryant, one of our earliest known ancestors.

Percy graduated from high school with honors, was the captain of his varsity basketball team, and was an Eagle Scout (only 22% of all Boy Scouts achieve this honor). Percy subsequently received a Bachelor's degree in Marketing.

Currently, Percy and a friend run their own nonprofit Basketball camp. The camp is tailored to young black men and focuses on 4 important aspects of life: 1) Academics, 2) Health and Nutrition, 3) Life Skills, and 4) Basketball Skills. Percy also volunteers with his local Big Brothers/Big Sisters organization.

Isabel Sarah Debnam

Outstanding College Student, Avid Cheerleader, Tutor, and a volunteer who works with Alzheimer's Patients

Isabel Sarah Debnam, the youngest daughter of Albert and Jaana Debnam, is the great-granddaughter of Rhoda and Albert Nixon. Isabel began her elementary education in Finland, but is currently majoring in Dietetics, Health and Wellness at a University in the United States.

Isabel played violin in the school orchestra in elementary school and maintained an interest in sports, particularly track. Currently, Isabel is a cheerleader at her college. Her team has placed in Stunt National Championships.

Isabel also tutors elementary school children with learning disabilities and also works at an assisted living facility. After college graduation, Isabel plans to complete a yearlong (required) dietetic internship in order to become a registered dietitian.

Michael Stanback

Multi-Talented Athlete and Exceptional Professional Barber

Michael Stanback, son of JoAnne Berry Stanback and Larry Stanback, is an all-around talented athlete who excels as an accomplished soccer player, a martial artist (Shalolin Wushu), and in his true love, basketball. He trained as a martial art's student for seven years, but he decided to switch to basketball full-time when he entered middle school. He played for the local Boys Club, and his team won the county division. Their final "All Star Championship" game for grand prize divisional win against a rival county occurred during the Washington Wizards half-time.

One of Michael's educational successes was when he received the highest score in English for his school's standardized Maryland School Performance Assessment Program (MSPAP) exam in 8th grade. He was in the honors program in high school where he initiated the Entrepreneurial Education Program for Apprentice Barbers.

Michael briefly attended a renowned Historical Black College in Atlanta, Georgia where he pursued a degree in Sports Journalism. He returned home to fulfill his entrepreneurial aspirations by becoming a self-employed professional barber. Michael quickly grew within the ranks at his barber shop and obtained his appropriate credentials via the state's Division of Occupational and Professional Licensing. He is now one of the most highly sought after barber's in the DMV for the past 11 years.

Presently, Michael is the personal barber for several NCAA (the National Collegiate Athletic Association), NBA and FIFA (Fédération Internationale de Football Association) players.

Matthew Stanback

Community Leader, Scholar, Outstanding Martial Artist Professional Businessman

Matthew Stanback, son of JoAnne Berry Stanback and Larry Stanback, at age five, began his martial arts training as a martial arts competitor in Shaolin Kung Fu at the Dennis Brown Shaolin Whushu Academy. Shifu Matthew also initiated the "Best of the Best Martial Arts School Entrepreneurial Education Program" along with Shifu Denard Spivey in 2004. Matthew was promoted to the managerial staff and was a lead instructor at age 15, teaching youth and adults. He trained under the direction of the following world-class athletes: Dennis Brown, Mfundishi Kijuana Vita, Jiang Bang Jun of the Beijing Wushu team, the legendary Oso Mfundishi Tayari Casel, Malenga Wallace Powell, Malenga Samuel Scott and his initial instructor and mentor Malenga Yusef Moore. Matthew now a fifth degree black belt has traveled to Beijing and studied with the Beijing Wushu team on several occasions, performed in Haiti, the Caribbean, the Wizard -Hawks half time show in Washington, DC and at Disney World, Orlando FL. In the past 24 years, he has won countless gold and silver medals and grand prize awards from tournaments throughout the nation. To date, Matthew is a staff instructor for the following classes: Executive Protection Training Courses, Health and Nutrition Assessments, Tien Shan Pai Kung-Fu and Tai Chi Training and Weight Loss and Fitness goals.

Educationally, Matthew is the recipient of two Presidential Awards (elementary and junior high school) for maintaining a 4.0 average for 8 consecutive years. He was also the grand prize winner for the 6th grade in County Science Fair. He is a graduate from one of the most prestigious, historically black colleges in Atlanta, GA with a degree in Accounting, Business Management (cum laude). While attending college, he participated in the following activities and societies: The Business Association, National Association of Black Accountants, Jumpstart for Young Children (Team Leader), Bonners Scholars Foundation, and is a Founding-Member of AUC Martial Arts Association Atlanta, GA.

Directly out of college, Matthew began working for one of the top fortune 500 companies in the United States as a Business and Planning Analyst, promoting to a Financial Analyst, Estimating and Pricing for over 7 years. He also obtained his masters from a highly noted Ivy League University in Technology Management and became a member of the City Lab Geneva Project. Presently, Matthew is employed for another fortune 500 company as a Senior Pricing Analyst.

Personally, Matthew cares deeply about his family and community and spends his weekends working with the youth and the disadvantage. He also recently married his beloved sweetheart, Rashidah, in December of 2015. Matthew was also the Master of Ceremony for the 2015 Bryant George Family Reunion.

Mom's Tribute and Thank You!

God blessed my brother Gerald and me with a phenomenal Mom who has lived her life serving God, family, and community. My fondest memories of my childhood found me surrounded by a large, loving family. In the 1950's, I witnessed the southern migration coming from the south. Our New York family members would provide safe lodging for those heading further north until they could establish employment and permanent housing. Everyone would gather over at the hosting relative home to greet our newly found family with food and fellowship. Cousins Lucinda Fox Ward, Fannie Alberta Peterson and Mom were the primary family organizers, each one of them were extraordinary and dynamic community leaders. Everyone supported each other's aspirations, community events, and church's activities, and of course, when anyone took ill our family came to their assistance.

On June 27th, 1976, Cousin Lucinda coordinated our very first family reunion at the New York Sheraton Hotel. The premise was to unite all who were related to her grandparents, Rhoda Bryant George and Edward Dudley George. Thus the Bryant George Family Reunion was launched. It was Cousin Lucinda's intention to further identify "who we are" as family members. Her quest developed over the years uniting almost all 9 branches of our family tree. Mom and Cousin Fannie Alberta Peterson, along with other family members, supported this effort. Amazingly, we have been celebrating our family tree for over 40 years.

When our beloved Cousin Lucinda transitioned on October 1st, 1984, Mom embraced the challenge to be our new family coordinator and held all the family branches close under wing. She was a true Shepard and didn't stop until we united with our Liberian family in the early 1990s. Our family focus was to support leadership, and each family branch would host a reunion which was ideal because we learned how diverse and unique we all are. However, one thread was evident, the profound talent and dynamic leadership capabilities we all possessed. We are comprised of a multitude of denominations: Christianity, Judaism, Islam, Jehovah Witness, and Catholicism. Over time, we also became a melting pot of different ethnicities: African, Jamaican, Hawaiian, European, Native American, and, of course, African-American. The same dynamics that prevailed from the earlier years have continued. We have maintained our connection, and thanks to technology, we know our rich family history even though we reside all over the world.

Mom has been an anchor for our family and the glue that has held us together. Her steadfast love for our family has never wavered throughout the years. She rises at times thinking of someone and within the week she would say, "I spoke to Cousins Mabel Rhoades, Fannie Fulcher, Sandra Fox or Ronda Bryant today." Please know, her list continued until she touched base with just about everyone. A true Shepard knows that each member of their flock holds importance and value. As I fully accept the new role of co-family coordinator along with my nephew, Albert Debnam, I am so very grateful to have had an exceptional and wonderful mentor in my Mom.

Mom, you have performed a valiant role in keeping our family history, values, traditions, and love for one another alive, and we collectively thank you for a magnificent job well done!

I love you endlessly Mom!!!

JoAnne

Author's Acknowledgements

I want to first offer my thanks to God for bringing into my life the persons who have helped make this publication possible. Without the many family members, friends, and people that God, in His divine providence, put in our lives at just the right moment and time, this book would not be ready to make its debut for all to see and read.

There are so many of you, family members and others, who have helped us put together the bits and pieces of this Bryant/George jigsaw puzzle. Many of you have prayed with us and have encouraged us along the way. To all of you, we offer our sincere thanks.

We recognize, even though they are no longer with us, Rev. Willie Lewis Jones and his sister, Annie Jones Dudley. We are so pleased that Rosalie Jones, now about 97 years old, is still with us. These three family members started us off with their memories of our Bryant ancestors. To Willie, Annie and Rosalie we offer our deepest gratitude and thanks.

Lucinda Fox Ward stepped up and accepted the mantle to formerly organize us into the Bryant George Family Reunions. We salute Lucinda for her role and outstanding leadership in launching us and setting the stage for our success today. We also pay tribute to the leaders of our reunions who have kept our stories and faith alive as we learned together "who we are as family."

We further salute our friends who represent our native homelands of Sierra Leone and Ghana for their stories from across the seas.

It is with much pride and thanksgiving that we have one of our own, Michele Stanback, who edited Chapters One and Five of our book. She is a tremendously gifted writer as well as a multifaceted artesian.

I give thanks to my son, Gerald, who urged me to purchase my first computer, and who has had the patience of Job as I have attempted to learn how to negotiate this technology. He has continually answered my many calls for help, and his extensive library, because of his role as a Cultural Historian, has been at my beck and call.

I am equally indebted and offer thanks to my daughter, JoAnne, for her role in spearheading our family resource publication, "Yesterday, Today, and Tomorrow" which has been an invaluable help as I searched for family ties and other information.

I would never be able to give all the names of my family members who have given me that important nugget of information at just the right time; thanks for your help and prayers.

I must tell you about two persons who have been so helpful to me in the writing of this book, Bobby Green, who took me to the many places that I explored for information in North Carolina and Japheth Bruce, a young man who has become so dear to me. His knowledge of the computer and his patience and eagerness to assist have enabled me to complete the book at our desired time.

Accolades to the Members of My Team:
Lillian Rhoades and Jeannette Whitfield

I cannot put in words just how much I appreciate and love Lillian and Jeannette who have worked diligently with me throughout this project. They both are talented, terrific writers and editors who have given me just the right tweak at just the right moment to enable a passage to have new and deeper meaning.

Lillian joined at the onset of my writing when I was still conflicted as to whether to be a historian or a story-teller. She helped me to recognize that I could be both. Later, she and Jeannette agreed that storytelling should perhaps be the more dominant medium with history as an introduction or as support to the main theme.

They have both given their time, talent, and expertise, and I have learned so much from them. They are devout Christians so we have been in continuous prayer, asking God to support our efforts.

Lillian is a professional editor who prepares books and other manuscripts for publication. She also has sisters who are gifted writers, so it must be in their genes.

Jeannette, who is multilingual, has the ability to look at words and recognize that they need correction or that they are not appropriate for a given sentence. She also uses this wonderful ability to teach others at Sargent Memorial Presbyterian Church. Jeannette, an ordained Elder, is the organizer of the church's tutorial program for children and youth, and in addition, is the Coordinator of the church's SHARE Food Program.

I could go on and on sharing how much my editorial teammates contribute to the places in which God has anchored them, and I truly feel and know that without them our book, *Two Worlds, The Captives and the Enslaved*, would not be the comprehensive agent to tell the stories of our Bryant/George family that we now share with you.

The family is like a book . . . The children are the leaves . . . . The parents are the cover, that . . . Protective beauty gives.

At first the pages of the book . . . Are blank and purely fair . . . But time soon writes memories . . . And paints pictures there.

Love is the little golden clasp . . . That bindeth up the trust . . . Oh, break it not lest all the leaves . . . Shall scatter and be lost!

Jeannette Whitfield

I was a child of that Great American Migration (1915-1970) of Black Americans as described in Isabel Wilkerson's book *The Warmth of Other Suns*. My family moved from Mississippi to St. Louis to New York City. I grew up primarily in the area of Manhattan known as East Harlem. Some people are traumatized by change and travel. I loved it. Many of my friends' parents were from other countries and spoke languages in their homes other than English. In elementary school, one of my favorite songs was *Far Away Places*, and little did I know it, but those "faraway places with the strange sounding names" gave me a love of history and called me into a career of international service and development.

I am a proud product of New York City public schools, graduating from Bronx High School of Science. I also graduated from the College of Wooster in Ohio, spending my junior year at the University of Dakar in Senegal (Université Cheikh Anta Diop de Dakar). Graduate school saw me back in New York City at Columbia University for a Master's Degree from the School of International and Public Affairs.

I have lived and worked in Africa as well as North and Central America and the Caribbean. In addition, I have traveled in South America and throughout Europe. I am multi-lingual. I say two things about myself: "I've rarely met a book I haven't wanted to read (at least in part) and rarely known of a country or place I wouldn't someday like to visit."

Lillian Rhoades

Lillian Rhoades is one of eight known grandchildren of Sallie Anne George and Anthony Rhodes and the third daughter of Arthur and Mabel Allen Rhoades.

Her writing skills were evident at an early age, and she succeeded her older sisters, Miriam Elizabeth and Virginia Sally Ann, as editor of the *Patrol*, their junior high school newspaper. Lillian graduated from New York City's Washington Irving High School and attended City College for two years before deciding to enter Brooklyn College School of Nursing. After obtaining a degree in nursing, she attended Nyack Missionary College (Nyack College) for two years.

Lillian practiced nursing for more than thirty-five years. She worked as a clinical nurse in several New York City hospitals, and later as a school nurse in upstate Rockland County, N.Y. During those years, she helped to establish The Soul Saving Station's Boy's Home in Mahotier, Haiti and raised two adopted sons, Tod Terrell and Shaun Bernard. After she retired and her "nest" was empty, Lillian wrote *When Youth Fades*, a book that tackled the subject of aging from a Christian perspective. Published in 2010, readers declared it "a gem," and "entertaining." One reader commented, "I guess this proves we are all aging.... which is what makes this book relevant."

Lillian is a consummate writer and her collection of poems and articles are not only impressive but extensive. Some of her works have appeared in magazines like *Essence* and the *Evangel*. Recently, two were in *Mixed Blessings*, a book that was published in 2015 by Breath of Fresh Air Publishers.

Our Author

Rhoda Carrison Nixon, daughter of William and Susie Carrison, is the granddaughter of Rhoda and Edward Dudley George, two of our earliest known ancestors. Rhoda, a native of North Carolina, received her earlier and higher education in Washington, D.C. She graduated from Dunbar High School, received a Bachelor of Science degree from Miner Teachers' College, and a Master of Social Work degree from Howard University. She later received additional training in Social Work Supervision and Administration from the New York School of Social Work and Fordham University.

Rhoda worked in various disciplines of social work and became certified as a Social Worker for the Bureau of Child Guidance - an evaluation, placement, and support unit of the Board of Education. Her innovative work with student social workers from Smith College and New York University led to the development of special techniques in social work education: a paper regarding this accomplishment was published by her Bureau.

Desiring advancement, Rhoda took and passed the New York State test for Supervisors and was placed on its waiting list. However, by the time her name was reached, the list was terminated. In the 1970s, this often was the practice whenever a number of minorities were eligible. Rhoda's determination and lobbying efforts to obtain equal employment rights for herself and other minorities led to legislation which provided for the subsequent hiring of minority Social Work Supervisors at the Board of Education.

Later, Rhoda, on loan from the Child Guidance Bureau, served as Assistant Director on a team charged with lobbying, planning, and establishing a drug prevention program called SPARK (the New York City School Prevention of Addiction through Rehabilitation and Knowledge) in all five Boroughs of New

York City. Rhoda subsequently served as SPARK's Staff Program Supervisor for the Borough of Queens. Her last Bureau assignment was to serve as Administrator, representing the Bureau of Child Guidance for School District 29, Queens. Rhoda's unit was comprised of forty-two workers who represented various mental health disciplines. Rhoda retired from the Bureau of Child Guidance after twenty-one years of service.

Our author then turned her attention to working more closely with the Presbyterian Church where she had served as Deacon, Elder, and Christian educator. In this new role, she was the Associate in Christian Education for New York City and Long Island Presbyteries, and she brought to their local churches a new style of innovative Christian education methods for urban ministry.

Most remember Rhoda for her work with New York City's youth project, called "The Youth Connection.' Supported by the New York City Presbytery and the Synod of the Northeast, she created this urban youth component. Rhoda's vision brought together a cluster of over 25 multiracial churches to become a support group for one another. It was because of Rhoda's deep commitment to young people that she recognized the need for New York City youth to have a Christian support system. This project offered spiritual development, leadership training, and personal development to over 300

young people. Rhoda called upon church leaders and teachers to join her in the formation of a Christian Education Committee to supervise the program. Financial and other resource help was given from Synod and National Presbyterian services. Young people had an active role in their program which offered: monthly visits to churches, retreats, workshops, visits to colleges, and a newsletter called "Keeping on Track" which was published monthly.

Later, when Rhoda was selected to be a writer for a Christian education mini-course for older youth, her effort, "Journey to Liberation" featured her "Youth Connection" program and was published in 1988 for five denominations, including her own, by Presbyterian Publishing House, Atlanta/Philadelphia. The Christian Education Committee celebrated Rhoda's successful tenure as NYC Presbytery's Associate in Christian Education with a Tribute at Riverside Church, NYC.

After leaving the New York City Presbytery, Rhoda taught courses in social work at the College of New Rochelle, NY and at New Brunswick Seminary. Part of the motivation for teaching at these institutions was to determine her next career move. Rhoda had been struggling with a call to become a minister.

After the first quarter of teaching, Rhoda realized that she no longer needed to resist God's call. She then entered New Brunswick Seminary as a candidate for ministry.

After receiving her Masters of Divinity degree, Rhoda relocated to the Washington, DC area and continued the process toward ordination. She subsequently was ordained in 1991 as Minister of the Word and Sacrament. She then accepted the call to serve as Associate Pastor and Minister of Evangelism at Adelphi Presbyterian Church in Adelphi, MD. Her work at Adelphi also included serving Beltsville Presbyterian Church, in an effort to determine whether the two congregations were a good fit to be merged. At both churches, not only did she preach God's word, but she brought her social work and evangelistic training to bear as she worked with her congregations.

After several years of working at Adelphi, Rhoda retired from ministry, but not from the calling to serve God's people. As is the custom in the Presbyterian Church, after formal retirement, Rhoda served as Parish Associate at Sargent Memorial Presbyterian Church in Washington, DC. She also served the National Capital Presbytery as Chairperson of the Evangelism Committee.

Rhoda's early community activities include founding the Educational and Emotional Growth Organization, Inc. (EEGO) which worked with community groups and the Board of Education. On a personal note, while at Miner Teachers' College, Rhoda organized a friends' auxiliary called the Amicae of Washington, DC which became an integral part of Zeta Phi Beta Sorority. Rhoda also organized and co-chartered a graduate chapter of her sorority, Delta Beta Zeta Chapter of Queens New York and became its first president. Currently, she is a member of Beta Zeta Chapter of Washington, DC.

Rhoda was blessed to have had a loving and devoted family. Albert, her husband of 23 years, now with God in eternity, was the wind behind her sails. Their four children, nine grandchildren, and eight great-grandchildren made their lives complete. Albert and Rhoda have been godparents and surrogate parents to a host of folks whom they have welcomed into their home and hearts over the years.

Rhoda gives honor and praise to God who defined her journey and has blessed her travel for 91 years. To have accomplished this lifelong venture of writing this book was made possible only with God as a covenant partner. This book is now Rhoda's gift to her Bryant/George family so that the stories of the past will not be lost but will live on through them.

www.ingramcontent.com/pod-product-compliance
Lightning Source LLC
Chambersburg PA
CBHW070547010526
44118CB00012B/1254